EXO

EXO
K-Pop Superstars

ADRIAN BESLEY

Michael O'Mara Books Limited

*For Nora, whose love of EXO and K-pop
is boundless*

First published in Great Britain in 2019 by
Michael O'Mara Books Limited
9 Lion Yard
Tremadoc Road
London SW4 7NQ

A CIP catalogue record for this book is available from the British Library.

Papers used by Michael O'Mara Books Limited are natural, recyclable
products made from wood grown in sustainable forests. The manufacturing
processes conform to the environmental regulations of the country of origin.

ISBN: 978-1-78929-114-8 in paperback print format
ISBN: 978-1-78929-115-5 in ebook format

1 2 3 4 5 6 7 8 9 10

Designed and typeset by Mark Bracey
Cover design by Ana Bjezancevic
Cover images: Imaginechina/REX/Shutterstock

Printed and bound by CPI Group (UK) Ltd, Croydon, CR0 4YY

Follow us on Twitter @OMaraBooks

www.mombooks.com

CONTENTS

INTRODUCTION

There's absolutely no doubt that when EXO exploded on to the stage to perform 'Power' at the closing ceremony of the 2018 Winter Olympics in Pyeongchang, South Korea, their high-energy performance made an incredible impact and won the group legions of new fans. However, EXO were already stars – not just in their members' home countries of South Korea and China, but across the world too.

Their hit singles 'Growl', 'Call Me Baby', 'Monster', 'Ko Ko Bop', 'Universe' and 'Tempo' have topped the charts everywhere from South East Asia to the Americas, Europe, Australia and the Middle East, and each of their five albums has sold over a million copies; their most recent, *Don't Mess Up My Tempo*, went to number one on the iTunes album charts in forty-six different countries.

EXO are hugely popular, but they weren't an overnight sensation. They've had to deal with disappointment, hardship and even scandal, but their success is a result of their wealth of talent, their willingness to work hard and the continual support of their management company, SM Entertainment. However, as EXO themselves are the first to admit, none of their triumphs could have happened without the love and dedication of EXO-Ls.

These are the fans who stood by them during their dark days, who sell out their concerts in record time, and who chant, wave their light sticks and hold up banners declaring their love at every performance. These are the fans who send video view-counters into the millions and EXO's music to the top of the charts. There are now more than 4 million official EXO fans worldwide and, via social media, EXO-Ls have come together as a genuine community. They help each other, support charities in the group's name and make lasting friendships as they follow the boys' ongoing success.

Every EXO-L has their 'bias' (favourite). For some it's the charming and articulate Suho, the group's leader; for others it's the *maknae* (youngest member), the eternally stylish Sehun; or the rapper and multi-instrumentalist Chanyeol, the self-appointed 'happy virus' of EXO. His fellow 'beagle liners' (a K-pop term for mischievous band members) – the ultra-handsome Baekhyun, and Chen with his infectious smile – have more than their share of devotees. Other fans favour lead dancer Kai, who just oozes sensuality; D.O., who has the softest eyes and perfect heart-shaped lips; Lay, the sole Chinese member, who just slays with his killer dimples; or Xiumin, the eldest, who, once considered a cute boy, is now a ruggedly handsome man.

However, as is evident in interviews and TV variety-show appearances, each of these boys has his own unique charms, and all are supremely talented individuals, rated among K-pop's very best vocalists and dancers. Some are songwriters in their own right and some are also acclaimed actors, while others have had hits as soloists or duetted with other artists. In dedicated chapters covering each of the nine members in turn, this book captures the personalities and achievements of each one.

EXO have a reputation for pushing boundaries. They are musical chameleons with a sound that is impossible to pigeonhole. Their recordings feature elements of R&B, EDM, hip-hop, tropical house, trap and pop music, and on their albums emotionally charged ballads sit beside funk-fuelled stomps, with melodious tracks enlivened by exquisite harmonies, catchy choruses, refreshing raps and, occasionally, unusual chants and yells.

But all this would stand for little without the stunning performances that bring the songs to life. Each time EXO reveal a comeback on the Korean TV music shows their singing is pitch-perfect, their incredibly complex choreography is completely on point, and they look awesome. That doesn't happen without weeks if not months of preparation, but

EXO always give their all. This book highlights some of their famous live routines, which you can find on YouTube and other online video sites.

A concert is all this multiplied by a hundred: a two- to three-hour extravaganza featuring thirty or so songs, dazzling dance moves, solo performances, multiple costume changes, amazing backdrops and lighting, specially made videos and stage sets that enable the band members to walk right out into the crowd. The audience are part of the show too, their co-ordinated light sticks casting waves of colour across the venue. It's an emotional rollercoaster for everyone as the group genuinely bond with the audience, fooling around, playing games, chatting to them and picking out their favourite banners.

This book tells the extraordinary story of EXO. A story of how hardworking trainees were launched as a group of aliens with superpowers, transported to Earth from a far-off world called EXO Planet and split into two units: EXO-K and EXO-M. It tells of the merging of the two groups into EXO, the years of hard graft, all the way through to the impact of *that* Winter Olympics performance in front of a global TV audience of millions and a long-awaited comeback at the end of 2018. We follow them from debut through their setbacks and their successes, chronicling the relationship between the group and the fans.

EXO-Ls have certainly embraced the mythology, and perhaps some really believe EXO are extraterrestrial beings – the group are definitely super-talented enough – but there is one aspect of the story that EXO-Ls all agree on: EXO are truly out of this world.

ONE

THE PLAN

Former musician and producer Lee Soo-man had been creating hit K-pop acts for his company SM Entertainment since the late 1990s. His success rate was unmatched in the K-pop industry. He had launched acts such as H.O.T., Shinhwa and the solo artist BoA, as well as Super Junior and Girls' Generation. However, since SHINee had arrived on the scene in 2008 and f(x) a year later, SM had failed to successfully launch a new act. Some said Soo-man had lost his touch…

Lee Soo-man knew how K-pop worked. He had all but invented the genre. When he returned from a spell in the USA in the late 1980s, enthused by Michael Jackson and the MTV revolution, he found a South Korean pop scene that was beginning to change. Koreans were embracing American music – hip-hop, R&B and pop – and acts were integrating these genres into traditional Korean popular music. Lee Soo-man was the right man at the right time and he devised a system for creating (some would liken it to a factory and say 'manufacturing') pop stars that would also be adopted by SM's main rivals, JYP Entertainment and YG Entertainment, and other K-pop music companies.

> Lee Soo-man knew how K-pop worked. He had all but invented the genre.

The system works by recruiting the best young talent in South Korea (and beyond) and bringing them to the SM headquarters in the capital, Seoul. These teenagers live in dormitories with other hopefuls and undergo a gruelling boot camp of dancing, singing, exercise, diet regimes and English, Chinese and Japanese lessons. They are expected to keep up their education too, sometimes attending new schools in Seoul.

K-pop groups often have more members than their Western equivalents, because they offer fans a complete package of skills. They have specialist rappers, vocalists, dancers and even 'visuals' – members included for their good looks and magnetic stage presence. The management company selects their acts from their pool of talent and some trainees (EXO's Suho being one example) face long waits, watching their friends and sometimes new arrivals get chosen for debut ahead of them.

A leader, responsible for conveying the company's instructions and representing the band to the public and to their management, is appointed for groups. This is often the eldest (although that isn't the case with EXO's Suho) and each group also has a *maknae*, or youngest member. In EXO, that's Sehun. *Maknaes* are like the baby of the family and are looked after by the other members. They are cute and adorable – and, like younger siblings, can get away with being cheeky and mischievous.

The company also assembles songwriters, producers, choreographers, image consultants and managers. When trainees are selected to be launched as a soloist or a group, these professionals take over and attend to every detail. The official launch is known as the 'debut'. This can take place at a special showcase, but often happens on one or more of the TV music shows.

SM Entertainment have created act after act with on-point choreography, stage presence, stunning outfits and good looks. All have been designed to impress, not only on the music shows but also on Korean TV variety shows – which sometimes involve interviews and performances but more often focus on amusing challenges that highlight artists' character, skills, humour and all-round ability to entertain.

Lee Soo-man is an astute marketeer. He creates a receptive audience for his acts' debuts, preparing the ground by releasing teaser photographs of members, setting up social-media accounts, posting preview performances and communicating with new fans. Then, if the debut is successful, he masterminds their 'comeback' in the same meticulous fashion. A comeback doesn't mean an artist remains dormant for a time or even necessarily takes a break; it's the term for their next launch, which often has a new 'concept' – a subtle or even major change in image or sound.

In Korea, Lee Soo-man's nickname is 'The President of Culture' because he spearheaded the musical aspect of the 'Korean Wave', or *hallyu*, the spread of Korean culture beyond the country's borders, cleverly utilizing social media and the growing profile of YouTube to make SM acts accessible across the rest of Asia and around the globe. In 2010, with SM Town Live, he took the company's star groups to perform in the USA, Japan, China and even France, and this was to be the basis of his new plan.

In 2011, Lee Soo-man gave a speech at Stanford University's Graduate School of Business in California. To a packed audience he explained how Korean pop was beginning to appeal to audiences around the world. He talked about recent SM Town Live concerts and mentioned a new project. SM Entertainment were about to launch two groups with the same, as-yet-undisclosed name – one consisting of South Koreans and the other of Chinese members. 'We plan to launch the group simultaneously in Korea and China,' said Soo-man, 'singing the same song in two different languages.'

Understandably, this created excitement online. SM were launching a new group! Rumours buzzed around the internet, but SM remained tight-lipped. It was months later, on 22 December 2011, that SM finally

> SM Entertainment were about to launch two groups with the same, as-yet-undisclosed name – one consisting of South Koreans and the other of Chinese members.

updated their official homepage with a twenty-four-hour countdown teaser featuring a hexagonal EXO logo, a galaxy of stars containing a planet emblazoned with the same logo and the words 'From EXO Planet'. The following day the new acts, EXO-K and EXO-M, were finally announced. They were described as 'new boy groups who will lead the world music industry from now on!' and (as Soo-man had indicated) they were to debut on the same day, at the same time, with the same song, in Korea and China respectively.

On 23 December, a short YouTube clip titled 'Teaser 1_Kai' revealed a charismatic and handsome dancer performing sharp moves to a bluesy, R&B track, which was later identified as 'My Lady'. Now fans sat up. Within forty-eight hours the video had amassed thousands of views. Four days later, Kai reappeared alongside another dancer, Luhan, performing to a track with more of a hip-hop vibe called 'Time Control'. The next day brought Tao, who delivered an exciting and acrobatic martial-arts performance. In conjunction with each introduction, photos of the latest member were uploaded to the website. Fans were drawn in, but confused. Why were they seeing so much of Kai when so few members had been revealed? Were all these tracks going to be released at debut? Were martial arts going to be a feature of EXO?

On 29 December, another new member was spotted as Chen appeared with the three others in a cute photo of them lying together on a bed. Later that day, they were all seen on the annual TV show *SBS Gayo Daejeon*, which translates as 'Korean Pop Music Festival', alongside other more established SM stars. Tao once again stunned fans with his martial-arts dancing, performing alongside Victoria from f(x), and Kai and Luhan danced with SHINee's Taemin and Super Junior's Eunhyuk. Then, in the SM Orchestra section, Chen revealed his gorgeous vocal ability for the first time and all four joined the more experienced SM stars in a finale. Was this EXO? No one knew for sure, but they had certainly made an impression and, online, fans speculated that the debut would surely come soon.

As 2012 began, more Kai teasers emerged. He certainly seemed to be the face of the group. Although there was no doubting his dancing talent and good looks, some questioned SM's fixation with him. The seventh teaser, however, piqued more interest, as Sehun was introduced alongside Kai. The pair danced, one in white trousers and a glitter jacket, the other wearing the opposite, and huge shadows followed their every move.

Teaser eight, released on 10 January 2012, was a game changer. It was a Sehun teaser, but in a shadowy reflection you could see a group photo with twelve members. This was the first full sighting of EXO! What's more, it had an instrumental backing track that fans flipped out over. Until now the music had been received relatively well, but people were waiting to see if, as SM promised, this new group could offer anything special. 'Black Pearl', an electro-bop that fans immediately begged to hear more of, was their answer.

Teaser nine upped the game again. Sehun and Luhan in an RV in a deserted world with two moons? There were vocals for the first time and again it was a song that connected immediately with those listening and 'Into Your World', which reappeared later as 'Angel', would forever be a favourite. Thousands were now locked into the teaser game. Each new clip was beautifully shot with a gripping soundtrack and seemed full of clues.

And they kept coming. Kai, Sehun and Tao reappeared, and by 24 January we had met Lay and Xiumin. Most groups have a handful of teasers before debuting. After a month, EXO had already posted twelve and we had made the acquaintance of only seven members!

Then, just as fans were becoming desperate, SM gave them something new to devour – a full track, complete with music video. The delicate and soulful ballad 'What Is Love' was released, as promised, in Korean and Chinese versions. Baekhyun and D.O., both yet to be introduced, sang on the Korean version with Chen and Luhan providing the Chinese vocals. 'What Is Love' really did the trick. Fans loved the soft ballad and, although some found the post-apocalyptic, sci-fi style of the video difficult to follow, they had fun picking out the previously unseen members. The Korean video even broke into the Top 100 on YouTube.

As teasers continued to appear every few days, fans couldn't help but be impressed by the quality of the music they were hearing, even if it was only in two-minute tasters. There were future favourites 'Two Moons' and 'Let Out the Beast', as well as clips of songs such as 'Phoenix', 'Emergency' and 'Metal' that never saw release but made an impact at the time. Meanwhile, SM were also periodically introducing new members, with D.O. and Baekhyun revealed as the eighth and ninth members at the end of January.

Teaser sixteen, released on Valentine's Day, saw D.O. and new face Suho in the most enigmatic video yet. In a desolate country setting, the two walk past each other apparently unaware of the other's presence. Suho sits at a table (in the middle of nowhere) while D.O. flies a kite carrying the EXO logo. A solar eclipse takes place (a recurring theme in many of the teasers) and at that point they seem to acknowledge each other. Nothing was made clear, but SM's inscrutable messages seemed to be deep and meaningful. The next day, Suho was introduced as the tenth member of EXO.

Now we met EXO member number eleven, Kris, who appeared alone in teaser seventeen – in which, as yet another eclipse unfolds, a god-like Kris, dressed all in white with a flowing cape, throws himself from the top of the building. On 21 February, Chen finally returned alongside Lay and Baekhyun, who appeared in his first and only teaser with another backing track, 'Beautiful', that demanded to be played on loop. Both of these featured more eclipses, but any complaints about confusing storylines were drowned out by those asking just how many cute young men SM could fit into one group – and how many great songs did they already have prepared?

There was one more member still to be introduced. The twentieth teaser was dedicated to Chanyeol and once again it felt heavy with symbolism, with him delivering a knowing smile as he experienced an eclipse alone in a dilapidated shed. Many declared the final member the pick of the good-looking boys, while many more were bewitched by the accompanying song, which was called 'El Dorado'.

Three more teasers followed, including Kai dancing to 'Baby Don't Cry', another song that would become a fan favourite. The line-up was now complete, even if there was still a lack of clarity about who was in which sub-group, but all soon became clear. Another pre-debut video was released on 9 March in two versions, with both the EXO-K and EXO-M versions featuring six members.

If fans had been getting tired of the endless teasers and frustrated by catching only snippets of potentially brilliant songs, 'History' wiped the slate clean. A high-octane romp packed full of mini-hooks with a fabulous chorus, it was the opposite of 'What Is Love'. The video backed up the story so far by placing all the members on an alien planet – and if the styling seemed slightly off, well, they were from another galaxy after all.

> If fans had been getting tired of the endless teasers, 'History' wiped the slate clean.

So it was official. EXO-K consisted of vocalists Baekhyun, D.O. and Suho, with Chanyeol in charge of rap, and a dance line of Kai and Sehun. EXO-M had a vocal line of Lay, Chen and Xiumin, with Kris rapping and Luhan and Tao dancing. Although many assumed all of EXO-M were Chinese, Chen and Xiumin were, in fact, South Korean, and they had the tough job of absorbing a new culture and learning Mandarin – quickly! Every K-pop group also needs a leader, and Suho, who had been at SM the longest, was selected to lead EXO-K, while Kris, the eldest of the Chinese members, was the leader of EXO-M.

It was March 2012. SM had put out twenty-three teasers and numerous photos featuring each of the members. Fans had lapped up EXO's two prologue videos and were ready for whatever SM had in store. Lee Sooman's plan was working pretty well so far, but the biggest test of all was just around the corner...

TWO

DEBUT

E ventually the teasing had to stop. It was finally EXO's turn to take to the stage for the K-pop rite of passage: debut. The dream of debuting is what motivates trainees in K-pop companies to endure the endless hours of rehearsals. It's an act's birthday, premiere and the biggest test of their young careers all rolled into one blast of high-adrenaline, high-profile events. It's their big opportunity to connect with the public and many performers, even those backed by big entertainment companies, fall at this first hurdle.

EXO-K and EXO-M's debut was revealed to be 31 March 2012 – exactly one hundred days after the first teaser had been released. This was no coincidence; a hundred days is a celebrated time period in Korean culture. *Baek-il*, as it is known, harks back to the days of high infant mortality when, once a baby had survived a hundred days, they were ready to be taken out and shown to the world: EXO's debut was to be their *baek-il*.

Of course, plenty of K-pop fans had already seen 'baby' EXO. The teasers had introduced all twelve members of the group and offered tasters of many of their tracks. Amazingly, these had amassed around 30 million views, arousing plenty of curiosity, excitement and passion – not only in South Korea and China but also elsewhere in the Far East, Europe, the Middle East and the Americas. The Olympic Hall in Seoul, the venue for their debut showcase, received over 8,000 applications for the 3,000 available tickets. No pressure then!

They were SM's first rookie group for four years, their company 'seniors' such as Super Junior and SHINee had set the bar extremely high, and no K-pop group had ever had such intense pre-debut promotion. Could EXO possibly live up to expectations? 'Of course, we feel pressured,' said Chanyeol in the showcase press conference. 'Our seniors opened the path well, so we're worried about whether we'll be able to live up to expectations... But I think that we work harder as the expectations on us get higher.'

It was Super Junior's leader, Leeteuk, who walked out on to the stage at the Olympic Hall to host the debut of a group that he had helped mentor through their trainee days, but even he couldn't have expected the ecstatic reaction from the light-stick-wielding, screaming fans as EXO opened the show with a live performance of 'History'. First EXO-K, then EXO-M, then all twelve of them together, filled the stage with synchronized moves and intricate choreography – it was hard to know where to look.

However, the audience were soon able to focus on the individual members of the group, from Kai, familiar from the teasers, dancing solo, to Baekhyun and D.O. almost stealing the show as they duetted on 'What Is Love', and Chanyeol and Kris facing off in a rap battle. Then all twelve ratcheted up the excitement with the first live performance of 'Mama'.

The next day, still buzzing from the audience reaction, they flew to China to repeat the showcase. This was a rookie group who were yet to debut, but hundreds of fans still met them at the airport. The show took place in the campus hall at the University of International Business and Economics in Beijing, a much smaller venue than the Olympic Hall, but there were only minor changes to the format and once again the audience brought the house down.

Over the following week, as SM put a recording of the Seoul show online and released the forthcoming album-cover photos, fans and the group had time for it all to sink in. On social media it appeared that Kai and Kris were pretty instant hits, the MV teaser had piqued interest, the vocal lines had certainly been stunning and fans were already lapping up the obvious camaraderie between the members, particularly when Luhan mentioned in the Q&A how cute the *maknae*, Sehun, was and how he felt he should look after him. Some felt that Suho should have featured in a teaser instead of making do with a montage of still shots, but the main concerns were for Tao and Kai, who both received injuries dancing at the Beijing showcase and had to be helped out of the hall.

An idol group can't truly claim to have debuted until they have performed on a major music show. After all the Facebook photos, the teasers, the prologue songs and the showcases, Sunday 8 April 2012 was the climax – the twin groups' official debut on TV. True to Lee Soo-man's plans, the two halves of EXO split to promote the group in separate countries. EXO-K were to debut on the TV music show *Inkigayo* in South Korea, while EXO-M would feature in a live broadcast of the Mengniu Music Chart Awards Ceremony in China.

Even six years later, Kai remembered how nervous they felt when they stood on the *Inkigayo* stage. They bawled out their 'We are one!' greeting and looked awkward and shy for their interview. D.O. famously stumbled over his description of their sound, describing it as a 'superior' instead of 'powerful' orchestra (the words start in a similar way in Korean) – a moment that he was unable to watch for a long time. When they got on stage to perform 'History' and 'Mama', though, they were step-perfect in the choreography, injecting energy and drama into the dance. They looked pretty good too, in black-and-white leather jackets and skinny jeans embellished with silver and glitter, and the fan chants in the studio were audible even above the music. Here was a debuting group with a ready-made fan base.

Over in China, EXO-M – similarly decked out in black and white but toned down slightly for the more conservative Chinese market – were giving the same flawless performance in front of an enthusiastic audience. Although the interview section was brief, it did include Kris firmly setting the MC straight after she told fans it was no use yelling as EXO-M couldn't understand Chinese; and later the audience got a snippet of Luhan's impressive voice when he sang a couple of lines from top Chinese artists Yu Quan's hit song 'Most Beautiful' as the veteran stars received an award.

With all the hype of the hundred-day launch, it was inevitable that some would find fault with the debut. 'Is that it?' said some underwhelmed observers, while others noted bitterly that the group had lip-synced their performances (probably a good move considering how nervous they were). EXO-K themselves were disappointed with their first live broadcast as they had struggled with their earphones and following the cameras. However, their response was to practise hard and take advice from their SM seniors.

> With all the hype of the hundred-day launch, it was inevitable that some would find fault with the debut.

Super Junior's leader, Leeteuk, emphasized that they needed to be close as a team, while TVXQ's Yunho, despite being in Japan, called them on speakerphone in their dressing room after their *Inkigayo* performance. 'He told us to sing on our run every morning,' said Baekhyun. 'We did and it really made a different to our live performances.' Super Junior would also present EXO-M with a big-time experience later in April when they invited them to perform as special guests at their concert in the 20,000-seater Mata Elang International Stadium in Jakarta, Indonesia.

By the end of the weekend, both EXO sub-groups were up and flying, and 'Mama' had been released as a digital single and music video in both Korean and Mandarin. Written and produced by SM's in-house hit-maker Yoo Young-jin, 'Mama' was used in the Korean sense of

'Your Majesty' and was no hymn to motherhood but instead a cry to a supreme being, Mother Nature, asking why our communication is so shackled to the digital world.

In similar versions for each sub-group, the video delivered EXO to the world in six epic, high-drama minutes. It starts with a sophisticated animation featuring a booming narrator telling how, under threat, the twelve forces of EXO Planet's Tree of Life were divided into two and hidden until the time when they would come together and 'a new world shall open up'.

The video proper reveals the boys dressed as monks performing a Gregorian-type chant that turns out to be not Latin but almost English – an anguished cry ending in 'No one care about me'. It then cuts effortlessly back and forth between several locations, including a desolate rocky landscape, a stylish sci-fi city, a super-modern cavern and a futuristic rooftop. The outfits are cool, the choreography is slick and the special effects and set changes left viewers open-mouthed.

As the song builds to a climax, the choreography steps up a gear, kicks and jabs flying in perfect synchronicity, before a passionate, almost heavy-metal-style scream interjects. In the EXO-K version it comes from a scary and possessed Kai, his face tattooed with the band's logo, the words 'EXO from EXO Planet 2012' and the names of the group's members, while, with more subtle face paint, a zombiefied Xiumin and an alien-styled Kris serve as EXO-M's designated screamers. The video plays out with the monks now exiled to a modern cityscape.

Some – including many of the group – found the manufactured mythology slightly uncomfortable, but, to give SM credit, they did it properly, and the video has class and quality. Everyone took a breath. EXO had landed with a video that was bursting with energy and style: the haters would have to dig deep to find fault there.

EXO had landed with a video that was bursting with energy and style: the haters would have to dig deep to find fault there.

'Mama' was the lead track on both sub-groups' debut EPs of the same name, released on 9 April 2012. As a statement it was ambitious and grandiose. An epic track that used a thumping drum beat to drive the song from the chanted opening through a string-based classical sound, a fast pop feel, a dubstep-type chorus, rap and even some metal – all the time maintaining a catchy melody. For EXO-M, Chen stood out with some great vocals while for EXO-K, D.O. and Baekhyun were getting noticed for their voice work.

The EP also featured the pre-debut tracks 'What Is Love' and 'History' along with three other songs that had briefly featured on various trailers. The soothing mid-tempo ballad 'Angel' (also known as 'Into Your World') was another showcase for EXO's vocalists, with Suho delighting EXO-K fans, and Lay and Luhan standing out in EXO-M's slightly more delicate version. The simple but catchy rap 'Two Moons' (which tied into the EXO mythology) found EXO-K borrowing Key from SHINee for the English part, while Xiumin's chorus gave the Chinese version a great mellow feel. To complete the EP they turned fully pop with 'Machine', a full-on boyband track that remains a fan favourite to this day.

As both groups continued to promote themselves on music shows, attention turned to the charts to see how the releases had fared. In China, EXO-M hit number one on the Sina Album Chart with 'Mama' going to the top of several singles charts. In Korea, EXO-K saw their EP go to number one on the Korean Gaon Album Chart and it debuted at number eight on the *Billboard* World Albums Chart. While 'Mama' didn't make a significant impact on the competitive Korean charts, it reached number seven on YouTube's Global Chart, so EXO-K had clearly made a mark internationally.

Years later, EXO's debut became the source of some debate. At various times both fans and 'antis' (those critical of the group on social media) have labelled them 'debut flops'. Certainly, a lot of money was spent on them pre-debut and they were hyped to the sky, but being SM Entertainment's chosen ones also led to some animosity from people who believed EXO had an unfair advantage over other groups. They were waiting to label EXO as SM's first and worst mistake; and, for those looking to snipe, whatever EXO achieved on debut would never have been enough to justify the hype.

On the other hand, when EXO finally became a supergroup, the accusation that they had been flops was used by some fans to create a myth. These boys, who were dismissed as *nugus* (an insulting K-pop term used to mean 'nobodys'), had worked and fought their way from obscurity to superstardom, and rising to such heights from such a disastrous debut gave their story a fairy-tale feel.

The truth is, of course, that the group had to debut under tremendous expectations, knowing they couldn't please everyone. They succeeded in creating a splash, making an impact on the charts and establishing a large fan base who adopted the name 'Exotics' (a term originating among international fans). They were not an overnight sensation, but what mattered to them at that moment was where EXO went next. Would EXO-M prove a long-term success in China? Would EXO-K win the coveted and all-important rookie prize at the end-of-year awards shows? And would a new full-length album give them the accolades and success of their SM seniors?

THREE

KISSES AND HUGS

K-pop has its own conventions. Debuts, music shows, award shows and comebacks all punctuate the careers of K-pop acts. EXO had stretched the concept of a debut with their extravagant teaser campaign and pre-debut singles, but, now that the EXO flag was up and flying on either side of the Yellow Sea, fans knew what to expect. Right? Well, not exactly...

Throughout April and May 2012, the twin groups continued to promote the EP in South Korea and China. As well as flying out to guest on Super Junior's big shows in Indonesia, EXO-M were interviewed on Chinese TV shows, including the incredibly popular variety show *Happy Camp*, which attracts tens of millions of viewers. Filmed in Lay's hometown, Changsha, it revealed the boys at their most relaxed yet. Lay was the focus of much of the fun, but the others joined in as they played binocular football, were tested by the 'ugly meter' app and displayed their talents, from Kris's catwalk strut and Tao's martial-arts dance to Xiumin pulling a *baozi* (dumpling) face.

Meanwhile, EXO-K were working hard covering all the Korean weekly music shows, singing live on some, and attending fan signings across the country. In the ultra-competitive world of K-pop, the post-debut period is a difficult time. The group has to try to maintain the momentum of the debut, keep a high profile and gain new fans, but the popular variety shows in South Korea, such as *Weekly Idol*, are dominated by existing groups.

EXO-K did, however, secure an appearance at the Dream Concert, an event that takes place every year at the Seoul World Cup Stadium in front of 35,000 fans. With groups such as TVXQ, 2PM and Girls' Generation sub-unit TTS headlining, EXO-K were near the bottom of the bill, but they were the only rookie act invited to perform. For Exotics it was a chance to see them not only on stage wearing new suit-and-tie outfits, but also performing something new in the form of a cover of Super Junior's 'Sorry, Sorry'.

The promotions for the EP effectively drew to a close at the middle of May, but there was one more treat planned for fans. For the first time since their showcase, both EXO-K and EXO-M appeared together on stage on the *Inkigayo* music show.

At the end of May, the two sub-groups took part in their first joint fan signing with two hundred invited fans (although a thousand more gathered to see them), before they all set off on the SM Town Live World Tour alongside the company's top acts, including SHINee, Super Junior, Girls' Generation, f(x) and BoA. The first stop was Los Angeles for a one-off concert at the Honda Center in Anaheim. The boys managed

EXO [MAMA] @SBS *Inkigayo* 인기가요 May 20 2012

This special performance on *Inkigayo* was arranged as a thank you to fans who had supported them since their debut and purchased more than 100,000 copies of the groups' first albums. They might have introduced themselves with the 'We are one!' chant, but the two halves of EXO had been performing in separate countries since their debut. However, they exude so much confidence (even swagger – looking at you, Kai!), it's possibly the best TV performance of the song and there is a palpable feeling of power when all twelve members come together on stage.

to slip away for a group trip to Disneyland, but were back in time to play their part in the show, performing 'Mama' and 'History'.

Over the next few months the tour took them to Taiwan, Tokyo, back to Seoul and on to Jakarta. In each city, EXO performed only those two songs, but members cropped up elsewhere in the show. Sehun and Luhan both had opportunities to dance with SHINee; D.O., Luhan, Sehun and Chanyeol sang 'DJ Got Us Fallin' in Love' with TTS; Kris covered 'Like a G6' with SHINee's Key and f(x)'s Amber; and both Kai and Tao took part in dance battles.

The groups spent the summer performing at small festivals in their respective countries. It was a period of small crowds (it was reported that EXO-K were paid in rice for one show!) and hard work that's often forgotten by those who claim they were cosseted by SM. In October, both participated in *hallyu* festivities. EXO-K stayed in Seoul to perform in a concert to build excitement for the following year's Winter Special Olympics, while EXO-M returned to California for KCON, the exhibition of Korean culture where the highlight is a K-pop concert. Despite a bill featuring B.A.P, VIXX and NU'EST, it was Kris and the boys who received the most raucous welcome as they performed a short set and took part in a Q&A session. They ended the set with 'Mama', which K-pop website Soompi described as 'one of the standout performances of the night'.

> It was a period of small crowds and hard work that's often forgotten by those who claim they were cosseted by SM.

All eyes were now on the awards season – a critical time for any K-pop act. As SM Entertainment's protégées, there was immense pressure for EXO to mark their debut with an award. 'Since all of our seniors got the rookie award, we feel like we have to get it too,' said Sehun in one interview. 'We want to surpass our seniors' popularity.' The concern was, though, that over seven months had elapsed since their debut without a new release – would that count against them?

Although all awards are gratefully received, in K-pop some have more significance than others. EXO-K had picked up minor awards for 'Mama' and EXO-M had taken rookie awards in China, but the prestigious Golden Disc Awards, Seoul Music Awards (SMA), Mnet Asian Music Awards (MAMA) and Melon Music Awards (MMA) were the prizes they really coveted.

Internationally, MAMA are the best-known and the Best New Act Award was seen as a straight fight between B.A.P and EXO-K – with both groups' fans developing a fierce rivalry. EXO performed at the show and, in the real 'wow' moment of the evening, were joined by SHINee for their seniors' 2010 hit 'Lucifer'. Unfortunately, they didn't take home the prize. The only consolation for Exotics was that neither did B.A.P; to everyone's great surprise, it was given to indie group Busker Busker.

EXO-K also failed to pick up the Golden Disc or Melon awards for new acts. It was more fuel for the critics who seemed desperate to dismiss them as flops. Then, on 31 January 2013, at the very end of the awards season, came the Seoul Music Awards, a major event in South Korea, and the members were visibly thrilled as they strode up to the stage at the Olympic Handball Gymnasium to collect the New Artist Award. Suho beamed as he gave the thank-you speech – although, of course, he had to share the spotlight with Chanyeol, who delighted in looking after the trophy for him. If only he had known that before too long collecting SMA trophies would become something of an EXO habit!

EXO had cleared the first hurdle. They had completed their rookie year with an award, and along the way had gained valuable stage experience and picked up fans at home and around the world. But Exotics were beginning to get a little angsty. It was nine months down the line since EXO's debut. Most rookie bands would have had a comeback by now – an EP if not a full album. Fans knew that EXO had material – they had heard snippets on the debut teasers – yet as winter turned to spring there was no teaser, no countdown and certainly no photoshoots.

Going on a 'hiatus' is not unusual in K-pop. Acts take a break because of military service, to do solo work or simply to rest, but after a debut? This was what was wittily called the 'Airport Era' by some early fans. Eras are usually associated with comebacks and albums, but for Exotics this period was filled with fan photos of the boys at airports, YouTube videos from the SM Town Live tour and a brief cameo in the teen K-drama *To the Beautiful You*.

They say that what doesn't kill you makes you stronger and many believe this period was key to cultivating EXO fans' amazing loyalty and dedication. Rumours of a comeback would lead to excitement across social media, only for those rumours to prove unfounded. But the fans didn't give up. While other K-pop enthusiasts suggested SM were deliberately letting the group fade away or had decided they were not good enough for a comeback, Exotics stood defiantly by their idols.

> They say that what doesn't kill you makes you stronger and many believe this period was key to cultivating EXO fans' amazing loyalty and dedication.

Amazingly, the fandom grew closer and closer. They entertained themselves with fan fiction, artwork and creative videos. Memes went viral, especially those inspired by misheard lyrics. 'Roar like a buffalo' from 'Two Moons' became 'Roll like a buffalo'; Chen's 'Girl, I can't explain what I feel' from 'What Is Love' was taken as 'Gull, I can't explain what I feel' – cue a flock of seabirds – and, perhaps best of all, when Luhan's opening to EXO-M's 'History' sounded to English speakers like 'Listen, enjoy the mayo', it launched hundreds of mayonnaise gags.

It was into this fevered atmosphere of fun, creativity and heightened expectation that a possible EXO comeback track first emerged. In late February 2013, an audio track called 'Wolf' was uploaded to SoundCloud. It was a poorly mixed recording, but recognisable as EXO – and it took Exotics completely by surprise. Some were outraged. It was awful, they said, a terrible song sung out of tune. Then there was laughter, especially at the *saranghaeyo* (I love you) line – some claimed it sounded like Mickey Mouse had joined the group while others suggested that D.O. had to be drunk! Then a few fans began to say, Hey I quite like this. OK, it's rough and ready, but lots of demos sound like that.

And yet the wait still wasn't over. In April, EXO-M demonstrated just how far they had come in China by picking up the Most Popular Group Award at the thirteenth Top Chinese Music Awards and the Popularity Award at the country's Billboard Music Awards. EXO-K performed with them on both occasions and on 11 May the full twelve appeared again at the prestigious Dream Concert, held in front of 45,000 at the World Cup Stadium in Seoul. The twin groups did seem to be seeing more of each other, so could that mean…?

Hell yes. Four days later SM finally put Exotics out of their misery. The comeback was happening. They were releasing a new full album called *XOXO* (kisses and hugs with the hexagon EXO logo morphing into an X and an O – clever, eh?) and, instead of two separate groups, EXO would come together to promote both Korean and Chinese versions.

To celebrate the end of the EXO class's first year, they released two teaser yearbook-style posters with all twelve members dressed in school uniforms. The first poster showed them with neatly combed hair looking like well-behaved, straight-laced students, while the second poster portrayed them as mischievous pranksters, pulling faces, blowing bubble-gum (Chanyeol) and winking (D.O.).

> To celebrate the end of the EXO class's first year, they released two teaser yearbook-style posters with all twelve members dressed in school uniforms.

After such a long wait, Exotics basked in daily teasers of the boys as model students and high-spirited schoolboys. Three pictures of the members in uniform spelled out the group's name while, among the individual photos, Kai appeared with cornrows as he posed in his American football kit; D.O. looked like a real troublemaker about to throw a chair; Luhan posed on a ladder looking like he'd just painted a mural of the group; Baekhyun was marvellously geeky in his white specs; Kris pulled a snarl as he sprawled on his dorm bed; and Chen had apparently fallen asleep in his beanie with an open comic book lying on his chest. Awww!

Chogiwa! This roughly translates as 'I can feel it coming', but to fans it means a joke, something funny, a source of pride, a catch-all word for all things EXO. It is also the first word of 'Wolf', the comeback music video uploaded to YouTube on 30 May 2013. '*Chogiwa!*' was the initial response from many fans to the video and the track itself, but over time 'Wolf' has become known as the song that everyone says they hate but secretly listens to at night.

Fans bought into EXO; they loved the boys' looks, voices and their awesome dance skills. But, in trying to be different, SM had made things difficult. The video for 'Wolf' featured the most amazingly sophisticated choreography. It was devised by US dance maestro Tony Testa and, as Kris later revealed, took them months to learn – but the prowling around, looking tough and, well, wolfing it up made many fans cringe or perhaps, even worse, laugh. Similarly, the song blended rap, random singing and choruses to a dubstep backing. It was so much better than the leaked version – and catchy too – but the growling and high-pitched howling?

However, many people's perceptions changed when the twelve-man EXO took to the *M Countdown* stage on the first of their TV music-show promotions and simply blew the place apart. Their performance was epic and dramatic. They nailed the choreography and injected so much energy and charisma – and the fans played their part as well, with their clearly audible chants helping to create an incredible atmosphere.

For the next few days they continued to perform on music shows and after an *Inkigayo* show on 2 June they held a surprise fan meeting at a nearby park. Astonishingly, more than 2,000 fans rushed to greet them. EXO were most definitely back. The next day, 'Wolf' dropped as a digital single in Korean and Mandarin versions and physical formats of *XOXO* were released – a *Kiss* edition in Korea and a *Hug* edition in China.

The eccentricities and theatricality of 'Wolf' certainly gained EXO attention. The album, however, delivered what most fans wanted from the group: solid songs, varied styles and stand-out vocals. The beautifully sung, stripped-back 'Baby Don't Cry', the upbeat dance track 'Let Out the Beast' and the mellow closing track 'My Lady' were recognisable from the debut teasers, and didn't disappoint in their finished versions, while among the new tracks, 'Black Pearl', a song international fans took to their hearts, was a beautifully crafted, multi-paced, cool R&B number and 'Heart Attack' surprised by combining a mysterious, other-worldly ballad with an up-tempo, clap-along beat.

That ability to chop and change genres, from hip-hop to ballads to boyband pop and more, produced a captivating album, with any one of the above tracks being named as their favourite by Exotics at the time. After a week, *Kiss* was number one and *Hug* number two in the South Korean charts, *Hug* topped the Chinese charts and a combined version sat at the peak of the *Billboard* World Albums Chart.

Exotics' patience had been rewarded. They'd stuck with the boys despite the rumours and haters, and EXO had come good with an album that pleased their fan base, earned critical acclaim and proved immensely popular. As some liked to say back then: *chogiwawesome!*

SUHO

FACT FILE

Name: Kim Jun-myeon

Stage name: Suho

Date of birth: 22 May 1991

Birthplace: Seoul, South Korea

Nationality: South Korean

Height: 1.76 metres (5'9")

Position in EXO: leader, vocalist

Sub-unit(s): EXO-K

EXO superpower: water

FOUR

SUHO

The stylish and ultra-polite Suho is the leader of EXO. He represents the group in public and takes care of the members, even if that sometimes means keeping them in line. He is also a valuable member of the group in his own right: a singer with a silky-smooth voice, a superb dancer and a great performer. But success didn't come easily to him. Suho was a trainee for longer than any of the other members and at times he feared that he might never get to debut.

Kim Jun-myeon was born in Seoul in 1991. He grew up in the district of Gangnam, one of the wealthiest areas in the whole of South Korea, and when he debuted with EXO much was made of his supposed wealth. After all, he was from this chic area, confessed to liking golf and often treated the other members of EXO to meals. However, Jun-myeon has insisted that he and his brother, four years his senior, grew up in a comfortable but not super-rich environment: his mother was a teacher, while his father was an economics professor at Soonchunhyang University.

Jun-myeon is pretty smart himself. In an episode of the *Problematic Man* TV series in 2015, he admitted to being the cleverest member of EXO and when his middle-school records were shown it was clear he was achieving high grades. He was even nicknamed Um-Chin-A – 'the perfect son of your mum's friend'. His parents had high hopes for a career in business for him, but, by eighth grade, the young Jun-myeon was already answering 'celebrity' when asked what he wanted to be when he grew up.

His school records also show Jun-myeon was a born leader. He was class president of his elementary school and the vice-chairman of his middle school's student body. They don't mention his handsome looks, but photos and the recollections of classmates certainly bear witness. It was those good looks that caught the attention of an SM casting scout when they attended his school's dance-club competition – Jun-myeon was just a spectator but was invited for an audition!

He didn't take up the offer immediately, but a year later, with his parents' support, he decided to give it a try and passed the audition first time, joining SM as a sixteen-year-old trainee in 2006. The trainee's life is tough, combining studies with dancing and singing, but Jun-myeon worked extra hard, spending weekends and holidays alone in the rehearsal room, practising his dancing.

Jun-myeon's early years went well. He made many friends, including future K-pop stars Kyuhyun of Super Junior, SHINee's Jonghyun and Girls' Generation's YoonA. He was chosen to be a part of a Super Junior film called *Attack on the Pin-Up Boys*, made an appearance (along with Kai and Chanyeol) in a TVXQ music video called 'HaHaHa Song' and was even sent to China with Minho, later of SHINee, to learn Mandarin.

As time went by, however, Jun-myeon began to feel he was being left behind. Trainees who were younger than him or who had started training after him were making their debuts. Then, just when it looked like he was about to feature in one of SM's developing plans, he suffered a terrible setback, injuring his leg so badly that he would not dance for a year. Nevertheless, although Kai had to carry him up the stairs to the rehearsal rooms, he was determined to participate in whatever way he could.

Unable to dance, Jun-myeon looked to improve in other areas. In 2009, he was accepted into the Korea National University of Arts, majoring in acting. Of course, he threw himself into it. 'I would go to school, even on the weekends, and every night I would go to SM to practise. Because of those tiring moments, I found faith in myself, realizing I can endure anything, because I've overcome this.'

Finally, things were also picking up at SM. Jun-myeon had been included in Lee Soo-man's twin-group project and, as the venture progressed, he reluctantly withdrew from the university. Jun-myeon would now be Suho from EXO Planet with a superpower that gave him the ability to command water. After seven long years as a trainee, he was going to debut at last.

He would not only be singing and dancing in the group; his new name, Suho, means 'guardian' in Korean, and he would also be the leader of EXO-K. In K-pop, being the leader of a group is an important role. Leaders act as the go-between for the group and the company, are responsible for the wellbeing of the other members, and represent the group in press conferences, interviews and award shows. Suho, of course, took the job seriously. He sought advice from U-Know Yunho, who had been leader of TVXQ, and Super Junior's Leeteuk, who is still considered one of K-pop's great leaders.

> His new name, Suho, means 'guardian' in Korean, and he would also be the leader of EXO-K.

Suho's leadership is now highly rated too. The members describe how he bought them food when they were starting out and had little money, and how he instituted Saturday meetings to help build the group's team spirit. In public, he is always respectful and polite, and his award-acceptance speeches are heartfelt – and he never forgets to thank EXO-Ls.

His leadership qualities have led to Suho collecting new nicknames. He has been called 'Sunnouncer' (Suho + Announcer) or 'Esuhort' (Suho + Escort), but the name fans took to heart was 'Mom', especially after Suho used it himself. When Kris ('Dad'), leader of EXO-M, left the group, many fans likened Suho to a single mum left with a bunch of kids to look after. EXO manager Lee Seung-hwan backed this up, saying, 'Suho is like a mom who constantly nags… Whenever he nags, though, he always seeks out the member who might be upset and comforts them warmly.'

The persona that has emerged since debut can only have endeared Suho to fans. Beneath the sensible public face there is a sensitive young man. He was visibly shaken when members left the group and is not afraid to cry at times of high emotion – although he says he is still embarrassed about breaking down in tears during his speech at their first music-show victory!

If, on occasion, he seems over-earnest or looks slightly awkward, then that only adds to his appeal. Because Suho is a lot of fun; in some ways he's just a big kid. Kai has recounted how he pretended to be Jack Sparrow when they watched *Pirates of the Caribbean*, while Chanyeol has revealed how Suho would read manga comics and challenge the others to fights. He is notorious for telling 'awful dad jokes', for putting on *that* slinky red dress to perform Girl's Day's 'Something' at a 2014 SM Town Live concert and for being the quick wit who can come up with lines like, 'Since we arrived on Earth, we've actually lost our powers a bit. They only appear in our music videos.'

Then there is the man's elegance and poise. He looks like a prince, so much so that he has been likened to one of Korea's national heroes, Prince Yi Wu. Although Suho describes himself as a Buddhist, Koreans describe him as having a 'Church Oppa' or boy-next-door look, implying he appears sweet and innocent. Increasingly, though, he has a more mature style, wearing a suit with such ease, while his hair, in black, blond or red, swept back or parted, reveals a glorious forehead and to-die-for eyebrows. It is unsurprising that he has had countless modelling assignments, including a cover shoot for *Esquire* magazine in September 2016.

It is hard to stand out in a group as packed with distinctive vocalists as EXO is, but Suho's honeyed tones perfectly complement the voices of the other members. His lines help light up songs such as 'Angel',

'Promise', 'My Answer' and 'Baby Don't Cry' and his part in the a cappella bridge is one of the treats of 'Tempo'.

Suho was given the song 'Beautiful' as a solo on the Lost Planet tour and made it a fan-service special, walking to the stage edge before giving one audience member a rose and taking a Polaroid photo with her. But it was at the Love Concert in Seoul in 2015 – EXO's first-ever dome concert – that he really unleashed the power in his voice in a solo cover of Kim Jo-han's 'I Want to Fall in Love'. By the time of the ElyXiOn shows, he had combined the two talents, turning 'Playboy' (a song written by his friend Jonghyun from SHINee, who died while EXO were on tour) into an intense, off-the-scale performance.

> It is hard to stand out in a group as packed with distinctive vocalists as EXO is, but Suho's honeyed tones perfectly complement the voices of the other members.

Apart from 'Beautiful', which appeared on the 2014 live album *Exology Chapter 1: The Lost Planet*, Suho has yet to record any solo tracks for EXO, but he has featured in several other recordings. Some of these were soundtracks (OSTs), including the sublime 'Beautiful Accident', an OST for the show of the same name and a duet with Chen, and the sweet-sounding 'Starlight', an OST for TV drama *The Universe's Star*.

SM Station, which saw SM Entertainment releasing a digital single every week, gave Suho further opportunities. Before the 2016 Summer Olympics in Rio he joined Super Junior's Leeteuk, singer Kassy, composer Cho Young-soo and a number of former Korean Olympic champions on the uplifting 'My Hero'; and in February 2017 his solo track 'Curtain' marked the end of season one of the SM Station project. This was a jazz-tinged ballad sung to a simple piano backing and it showed Suho had the range and control to master a deeply emotional song.

Jun-myeon might have had to give up his university drama course when he became Suho, but he never relinquished his dream of being an actor. He did appear in various TV shows, including a successful

SM Station – Suho and Jang Jae-in – 'Dinner'

SM Station returned in 2018 and in March 'Dinner', a duet featuring Suho and singer-songwriter Jang Jae-in, was released. Over a muted instrumental, Suho's smooth tones blend so well with Jae-in's quirky, airy notes. In the video – a series of dark but beautifully shot scenes showing a couple's disengaged relationship – we also see dressed-up Suho at his finest. The pairing was a great success, with the song reaching number eleven in the *Billboard* World Digital Song Sales Chart, and the duo also featured on another track, 'Do You Have a Moment', released by Jang Jae-in's company, Mystic Listen.

nine-month spell in 2014 presenting the music show *Inkigayo* along with Baekhyun; a year later, he joined his friends Kyuhyun from Super Junior and Minho from SHINee, as well as other K-pop stars, in *Fluttering India*, a reality show exploring that fascinating country. However, his opportunities to actually act were limited to EXO videos, the SM 'hologram' musical (performers appeared as holograms, not in person) called *School OZ* and the slightly cheesy, albeit very popular, web series *EXO Next Door*.

This was to change in 2016, though, when he was cast in the movie *Glory Day* (aka *One-Way Trip*). Making his debut alongside a group of up-and-coming young actors, Jun-myeon (as he is still called when acting) was by no means overshadowed. TV roles followed for which he received good reviews. Playing a K-pop star in the romantic TV series *The Universe's Star* may not have tested him too much, but in 2018's *Rich Man* he excelled as the temperamental but witty Yoo-chan, CEO of a gaming company, whose disability prevents him from recognizing the face of the woman he loves. Jun-myeon's screen career has continued to prosper: in 2018 he starred in a movie called *Middle School Girl A*, and also landed the lead role – a genius pastry chef – in the forthcoming web drama series *How Are You Bread*.

Back as Suho, in 2017 he made his debut in musical theatre when he starred as Prince Rudolph (a role shared by VIXX's Leo and musical actor Kai – not EXO's Kai!) in the musical *The Last Kiss*. The role required a range of singing styles and tested Suho, but he was warmly praised for it. It was during his final performance in the show – just two days after the death of his friend Jonghyun from SHINee – that Suho broke down in tears during the closing scene.

In the audience at that last performance of *The Last Kiss* was Suho's bandmate Sehun, who is reported to have clapped and shouted Suho's name in support. The leader and the *maknae* might not be an obvious pairing, but they have long been good friends. They have holidayed together and shared a room in the EXO dorm for five years – Suho eventually leaving when a free room became available. However, when they appeared together on the *Hello Counselor* TV show, Sehun recalled just how messy his roommate was and Suho was forced to admit he had a problem with not being able to throw things away, even keeping clothes from his schooldays!

Those long days as a trainee at SM Entertainment served Suho well. He learned how to cope with disappointment and setbacks, but also gleaned so much from his fellow idols about how to be an effective leader. He has now spent as long in EXO as he spent as a trainee, and both his singing and his dancing have blossomed. He is an essential component in the EXO sound and choreography, and has always shown by example how a real leader looks out for their fellow members, representing the group with honour and dignity.

Those long days as a trainee at SM Entertainment served Suho well. He learned how to cope with disappointment and setbacks, but also gleaned so much from his fellow idols about how to be an effective leader.

FIVE

SHOWTIME

K-pop is competitive. Ultra-competitive. Record sales, downloads, YouTube views and awards are all studied to assess an act's status. The TV music shows reflect this. *The Show, Show Champion, M Countdown, Music Bank, Music Core* and *Inkigayo* are broadcast on different days and each presents its own weekly trophy based on varying aggregates of sales, downloads, panel surveys, social media engagements and even ringtones. For an award-winning rookie group like EXO, a music-show win is the next big hurdle.

EXO had been promoting themselves across all the programmes for two weeks when they took the trophy on the *Music Bank* stage on 14 June 2013. Their jubilant and emotional reaction showed exactly what it meant to them and, just as he had predicted, Suho was in floods of tears as he tried to give his acceptance speech. Amazingly, the next day they took another prize, this time on *Music Core*, and then again on *Inkigayo* on the following day. Three consecutive wins in a week – wow!

With 'Wolf' flying so high, EXO finally received their invite on to *Weekly Idol*, one of the top South

> The group had often appeared shy and nervous on TV shows, so how would they fare with hosts Jeong Hyeong-don and Defconn, who love to tease their guests, especially the shy ones?

Korean variety shows. The group had often appeared shy and nervous when promoting 'Mama' on TV shows, so how would they fare with hosts Jeong Hyeong-don and Defconn, who love to tease their guests, especially the shy ones?

The answer was they smashed it! From the opening section where the hosts guess who is in EXO-K and who is in EXO-M, to their tongue-in-cheek superpowers display, the boys, in their red-and-white Wolf 88 sports gear (88 is Morse code for hugs and kisses), were engaging and funny. They enthusiastically joined in the random dance segment (where they had to remember the choreography to parts of their songs), the special-skills section (Kai's impression of Squidward from *SpongeBob SquarePants* and Kris's cartoon drawing of host Defconn were highlights) and the 'sing the highest note competition' (Xiumin beat Chen and Baekhyun), as well as taking every tease in good spirit – even giving some back in return. It was so good that the episode received record viewer ratings.

In this and appearances on other variety shows such as *Beatles Code*, *After School Club*, *Star King* and the Chinese show *Happy Camp*, the public were at last getting to see the charming and talented boys that Exotics knew. July was busy with fan signings and performances on music shows, but SM had a card up their sleeve – and it was an ace. On 25 August, they announced a new single, 'Growl', as part of a repackaged *XOXO* album to be released the following week.

The music video for 'Growl' was uploaded on 1 August 2013, before the single and album were made available. For four days the only way to hear the song was by watching the video, but no one seemed to mind. Once again SM and EXO had pushed the envelope. In an original and daring step, they had shot the whole video in muted colours and in one take – a single camera shot that had no edits from start to finish. This meant no cut-away lingering close-ups or individual cameos, but it also meant that mistakes couldn't be hidden and the whole take had to be perfect. That's pretty tough in a dance video.

'Growl' isn't perfect, but it isn't far off – and the tiny errors (look out for Kai's hat falling off) just add to the authenticity. It was filmed in a strobe-lit, deserted warehouse-type building some claim was haunted. The boys are in their preppy high-school uniforms, which have been customized in various ways, from D.O.'s bow tie to Suho's armband and shorts, and Chanyeol's and Tao's sleeveless jackets, and they dance like their lives depend on it. The moves are cheeky, sexy and sometimes incredibly technical, but they're never flashy or extravagant, and it all amounts to spellbinding choreography and a superb video. EXO had revealed their true superpower: performance.

The song itself was what Exotics had been crying out for: something that stood out from the K-pop crowd but wasn't outlandish like 'Wolf' or, well, slightly weird like 'Mama'. It's a cracking pop tune with a hip-hop beat, a rhythmic chorus, a funky backbone and some damn fine vocals. In 2017, Jeff Benjamin, *Billboard*'s K-pop expert, included it in his list of the ten greatest K-pop choruses of the 21st century, praising its eccentric and experimental 'I growl, growl, growl' hook.

In 2017, Jeff Benjamin, *Billboard*'s K-pop expert, included 'Growl' in his list of the ten greatest K-pop choruses of the 21st century.

Before the track was released, the full EXO line-up also performed 'Growl' on music shows and by the time it dropped on 5 August, fans were well and truly primed. It topped nearly all the Korean digital charts within an hour, and went to number two in the Gaon Chart and number three in the *Billboard* World Digital Song Sales Chart. At the same time, the repackaged version of *XOXO* (renamed *Growl*) had been released, complete with the new single and two other new tracks, 'XOXO (Kisses and Hugs)' and 'Lucky'.

On the *Music Bank* show of 16 August, a month after their first ever win, 'Growl' notched up its initial triumph. By the end of the week it had bagged three more wins. And it didn't stop. A triple crown – victories in three successive weeks on a music show – is an honour achieved only by elite K-pop groups. 'Growl' picked up triple crowns on *Show Champion*, *Inkigayo*, *M Countdown* and *Music Core*, and only just missed the full set of shows when EXO were edged out on *Music Bank* by girl group Crayon Pop at the end of the month.

EXO promoted 'Growl' extensively in South Korea and it was played all over the radio, talked about on TV chat shows and obsessed about in schools across the nation. By the time the summer was over, everyone was familiar with the song, whether they were old or young or lived in the countryside or the city. A defector from North Korea even revealed that, although K-pop was banned there, 'Growl' was immensely popular and often used as a confession song – a chance for a young person to express their secret crush.

Promotions in China were less frequent. However, the group appeared to a raucous reception at the China Big Love Concert and the Nanjing Love Concert, and their popularity was confirmed when they picked up the Popular Group Award at the Asian Idol Awards. It was clear that fans there had really taken to the Chinese members. In fact, in an October 2013 Chinese poll to find Asia's Most Handsome Man, Kris and Lay came in the top ten and Luhan was the clear winner with over 40 million votes.

EXO at MAMA 2013

This November 2013 performance of 'Growl' and 'Wolf' is considered by some to be EXO's finest-ever live showcase. All twelve members appear in a great set with new choreography, and they really play to the cameras as well as the audience. Unfortunately, D.O. injured his ankle during the show and was rushed to hospital immediately afterwards, so sadly he wasn't around when something rather exciting happened later on that evening.

As the promotions drew to a close, the true extent of EXO's breakthrough became apparent. 'EXO LIVE! Growl on One Summer Night!', a live online event in which the boys performed and held Q&As, was streamed by 350,000 fans from ninety different countries. And a year after EXO-M wowed KCON in LA, the whole group travelled to the 2013 event. They performed a crowd-pleasing medley and took part in a great Q&A session, which included singing their favourite US hits. *Billboard* magazine noted that they had earned rave reviews from fans and KCON staff members alike for being the most outgoing, friendliest and funniest act at the fan engagements.

To cap it all, at the end of August they made a surprise appearance on *Infinity Challenge*, a peak-time, Saturday-evening light-entertainment show and one of Korean TV's most popular programmes. As one Exotic wrote online, '"Wolf" made EXO the talk of the town, but "Growl" made them the talk of the nation.'

SM had released dance-rehearsal videos for both singles, but the real excitement was saved for the two drama videos that were uploaded in the summer. To a soundtrack of their best songs, these short, linked pieces allowed the boys to show off their acting skills for the first time. The story focuses on Luhan, a new boy in school (or even on the planet), who seems attracted to Kai's girlfriend and manages to get his new friends (EXO) into a scrap with some toughs. The story manages to maintain the group's sci-fi connection, create an air of mystery and, of course, have plenty of stylish shots – especially of Luhan and Kai – with Tao performing some fine martial-arts combat.

Looking back, most fans just loved the baby-faces and innocence of

Billboard magazine noted that they had earned rave reviews from fans and KCON staff members alike for being the most outgoing, friendliest and funniest act at the fan engagements.

the group. Clothes-wise it was an era of fake fur and bandanas, but is remembered for Sehun's rainbow hair, D.O.'s iconic red backcomb, Luhan going blond and Baekhyun's poodle cut in blond and red. Probably best forgotten are Kai's cornrows, Lay's slightly strange flat, yellow locks and Tao rocking the emo style.

Opportunities to really get to know EXO had so far been fairly limited, but fans were about to be spoiled. November brought a new series, *Showtime*, broadcast over twelve episodes on Thursday evenings on cable channel MBC Everyone. *Showtime* was EXO's very own reality show and it had a great theme – the activities would be inspired by fans' questions. For many fans this was their first chance to see the twelve members away from the music promotions and it immediately proved incredibly popular.

The fifty-minute episodes allowed us to see them up close and personal as they took on challenges, went on trips, played games and spent plenty of time eating. As the series progressed, they became less shy and awkward (except for Baekhyun and Chanyeol – they were loud from the get-go!) and their characters gradually emerged. Probably most surprising was Kris, the supposed 'cold man', who turned out to be a real live wire.

EXO 'All My Loving'

EXO – well, a third of EXO – took to the stage on SBS's *Star Faceoff Chuseok Special* and impersonated The Beatles! D.O., Chen and Lay all rocked guitars while Chanyeol dominated the drums as they performed a cover of The Beatles' classic 'All My Loving'. Their voices were even distorted in order to make them sound like they were singing in the 1960s. Although their bowl-cut hair was hilarious, they looked really sharp in their suits and completely pulled it off.

Showtime stretched through December and over the Christmas and New Year period into February, providing Exotics with plenty of laughs, some gasps and some tears. Adventures included buying presents for Chanyeol's birthday, celebrating Christmas together, taking a tour of Seoul, exploring a haunted house and undergoing a telepathy challenge to see how in sync the boys were with each other.

EXO fans lapped it up. Kai and Suho went off the cute scale when they played with puppies; the vocal line rapped and competed to hit high and low notes in the studio; the whole gang (except sleeping Chen and Sehun, who was reading) cried through a Christmas movie; Baekhyun and D.O. brought Xiumin out of his shell in a special edition of their 'Most shabby talk show in the world'; and fans gaped at the final episode's thigh-wrestling competition.

Showtime also brought new words and phrases to the Exotics' lexicon. Kris became known as 'Galaxy Man' after giving the answer 'Galaxy' when asked where he would like to go with EXO (Lay's reply was 'to Baekhyun's grandmother's house', which was so sweet) and his 'Chicken is not my style' pronouncement entered EXO legend. Baekhyun debuted his own term, *kkaebsong*, meaning 'what a pity' – a word he would adopt again in the future. And we began to learn Sehunese as the *maknae* taught us 'Yehet', a sound he makes when he's happy or excited, and 'Ohorat!', his very own customized version of 'Alright!'

In the space of just over six months EXO had gone from being the forgotten debutants on a never-ending hiatus to the nation's favourites. Only Exotics were not surprised by the group's success. These dedicated fans had gained a reputation for their undying support of their idols (*Inkigayo* had called them 'crazy' when they banned them for their over-enthusiastic support). Now, their numbers were swelling as EXO became the number-one K-pop act in Korea and China, with an international fandom growing by the day. Everything was going so right. What could possibly go wrong?

XIUMIN

FACT FILE

Name: Kim Min-seok

Stage name: Xiumin

Date of birth: 26 March 1990

Birthplace: Guri, South Korea

Nationality: South Korean

Height: 1.73 metres (5'8")

Position in EXO: vocalist, rapper, dancer

Sub-unit(s): EXO-M, EXO-CBX

EXO superpower: frost

SIX

XIUMIN

There's something about Xiumin. Some swear it's his cat-like eyes, others his baby-face, his smile or his quiet, reserved charm. Whatever it is, it gets him noticed. Xiumin has been nicknamed the group's 'Muggle King' and labelled the *ipdeok* of EXO, both terms alluding to the way in which he makes people curious about the group and draws them into the fandom. When he heard about the *ipdeok* tag, he smiled and said he was honoured. That's Xiumin – polite and unassuming.

Xiumin stans may beg to differ, but his own assessment of his talents within EXO are equally modest. He doesn't believe he has the supreme dancing ability, vocal qualities or rapping skills of his fellow band members. However, he describes himself as someone who is able to bring out the best in others, the perfect foil, and, as his career has progressed, he has developed into a star vocalist and a rapidly improving rapper.

Despite joining SM Entertainment as a vocalist, singing was never a career choice for the young Kim Min-seok. He grew up in Guri, a city just fifteen minutes by car or train from Seoul,

> Xiumin describes himself as someone who is able to bring out the best in others, the perfect foil, and, as his career has progressed, he has developed into a star vocalist and a rapidly improving rapper.

and, although he likes to keep his home life private, fans have long known he has a younger sister (on more than one occasion he has mentioned that he would not want her dating an EXO member!). SM have also uploaded videos (still on YouTube) from his childhood. One shows an adorable Min-seok, aged around two, dancing in traditional Korean clothes, and in another he is the cutest toddler in a group dance – dressed as a penguin.

As a child he was a high-achieving student with consistently good grades. He enjoyed singing, but was really more interested in sport. He liked baseball and earned black belts in kendo and taekwondo, but his real love was football, a passion he still holds dear. In 2008, Min-seok decided to take an entrance examination for a physical-education college (he had already unsuccessfully auditioned for another K-pop giant, JYP Entertainment), when a friend persuaded him to enter the EverySing karaoke-style competition. He sang Emerald Castle's 'Footsteps' and came second, reportedly winning $1,000 and an opportunity to meet SM's casting team. Unfortunately, Min-seok's friend was not successful.

> There was one other reason Min-seok wanted to join SM. He was – and still is – a huge fan of SM band TVXQ and he loved the idea of being in the same company as them.

There was one other reason Min-seok wanted to join SM. He was – and still is – a huge fan of SM band TVXQ and he loved the idea of being in the same company as them. He soon became friends with the members, wearing their merchandise and even joining them on stage, but when he later appeared alongside TVXQ's Changmin on TV, he revealed how awestruck he was when meeting his heroes. Changmin seemed doubtful, joking that Xiumin complained his meat hadn't been cooked properly and seemed comfortable saying anything he wanted!

Min-seok started life as a trainee later in 2008. He would spend more than three years training before debuting with EXO. He didn't find the intense practice and long hours of trainee life as difficult as some, and continued to study, majoring in science and taking honours classes in maths at high school, where he was good friends with Infinite's Dongwoo. Performing was now a serious option and Min-seok put aside his other ambition of being an architect.

On 24 January 2012, Min-seok appeared in EXO's eleventh video teaser, alongside Kai. He was sharply dressed in a leather jacket, and black-and-white shirt and tie. His hair was dark, short and parted at the side to reveal his forehead and solid eyebrows. He looked confident and tough(ish) as the pair were chased by cars through the dark city. Two days later he became the seventh member to be formally revealed, as SM introduced Xiumin (usually pronounced 'Shoo-min' in non-Chinese speaking countries) from the planet EXO, whose superpower was the ability to turn things to ice. Despite being Korean, Xiumin was a member of EXO-M and would promote in China, singing in Mandarin.

Xiumin knew little Chinese and it must have been a difficult time for him. But you seldom hear Min-seok complain – although he did admit to feeling short, saying that after she saw his videos, his mother had told him never to stand beside Tao and Kris! He first roomed with Tao, and later with Kris and Luhan. A shared love of football brought him close to Luhan and it was he who gave Xiumin his first group nickname (he's one of those idols who attract nicknames), 'Baozi', which was eagerly taken up by Exotics. *Baozi* (also known as *bao*) are filled steamed buns, which are popular in China and sometimes known as Chinese dumplings in the West. Luhan said that when he first met Xiumin he thought him pale, white and squishy, and when Xiumin smiled his face became really round and he looked just like a *baozi*. Some fans thought the nickname unkind (Xiumin, of course,

> Luhan said that when he first met Xiumin he thought him pale, white and squishy, and when Xiumin smiled his face became really round and he looked just like a *baozi*.

never complained!) and campaigned for Exotics not to use it – though as his appearance changed over the years, it became less relevant anyway.

When EXO-M appeared with EXO-K another nickname emerged: 'Fake *Maknae*'. Tao was the EXO-M *maknae* (the youngest member) and Sehun the EXO-K *maknae*, yet Xiumin always looked younger and cuter than either of them. The image was helped by his sometimes childlike excitement and marvellous *aegyo* ability, but it is his delicate, almost feminine, features that made the difference. Indeed, many pointed out his resemblance to both girl group Mamamoo's Moon Byul and former Wonder Girl Sohee.

In fact, Xiumin is the eldest member of EXO. In Korean society, age is an important influence on how you behave and Min-seok is extremely well-mannered. By nature, he is also quite quiet – he is happy in his own company, playing videogames or watching a movie – but that doesn't mean he doesn't have a fun side; he has confessed that, particularly in the early days, the pressure not to play around or be mischievous with the younger members was sometimes difficult. Within the group, Chen and Xiumin have been best friends for years. In the V Live show *Travel Without a Manager*, Xiumin said, 'I don't think there are any others [in the group] who are as close as we are.' Chen added, 'He's like my brother,' to which Xiumin jokingly replied, 'And he's like my wife!'

Xiumin remained tight-lipped about the EXO-M members who left, and carried on working hard, but gradually fans learned more about the most enigmatic member of EXO. They discovered that he liked coffee, declaring an ambition to be a barista, and that he was partial to an alcoholic drink now and then too. Other members were quick to name him as the tidiest of them all. 'I get stressed when things are messy,' he admitted, 'so I take responsibility and clean.' He also continued his studies, enrolling at the Catholic Kwandong University and majoring in music. He has since graduated and is rumoured to be taking a doctorate programme at Hoseo University.

Fans also learned that Xiumin's childhood love of sport had endured. He is the strongest member of the group, winning all their arm-wrestling competitions, and is an accomplished and enthusiastic footballer. His skills became apparent in the 2013 Asian Dream Cup when he played for a Korean all-star team (which also included Manchester United's Patrice Evra) and whenever possible would play in the *Idol Star Athletics Championships* (an Olympic-style event for K-pop stars). He also threw the first pitch for baseball team LG Twins, a team he and his father had supported since he was a boy.

Initially, when Xiumin found himself back in a ten- and then nine-man EXO, he was perhaps overshadowed in recordings by the group's other vocalists, and his lines were often used as balance, but, as he grew in confidence, a smooth, silky vocal style emerged. There was certainly no hiding him on stage. His dancing just got better and better and he began to look more like a man than a boy. He lost those chubby *baozi* cheeks and he also put in the work on his body, developing some magnificent abs (which Baekhyun takes great pleasure in revealing at live shows).

When the sub-unit EXO-CBX emerged in October 2016, Xiumin blossomed. In songs like 'Rhythm After Summer', 'Juliet' and 'Playdate' his voice shines – and in 'Ka-Ching' he convinced fans that he really was a bona fide rapper. The fun videos he made with Chen and Baekhyun really allowed his personality to come through and there was absolutely no doubt that this man was a dancer; in many other groups, he would have been the lead dancer.

> The fun videos Xiumin made with Chen and Baekhyun really allowed his personality to come through and there was absolutely no doubt that this man was a dancer.

Outside of EXO, Xiumin has had a few noteworthy collaborations. In March 2016 he became the first person to collaborate with Jimin of girl group AOA in her Outfit of the Day project. Their single 'Call You Bae'

BeatBurger and Xiumin – 'Beyond' – EXO Planet #4 – The ElyXiOn [dot]

In EXO's ElyXiOn [dot] show, Xiumin was finally given his moment to shine and he grabbed it with both hands. 'Beyond' is Xiumin's collaboration with SM Entertainment electronic dance band BeatBurger and this performance was so good that they released it as the music video. All sides of Xiumin are on display here – cute-as-pie Xiumin, dance-machine Xiumin, super-sexy Xiumin, sweet-vocal Xiumin – but it's best for watching Xiumin have the time of his life doing what he does best: performing.

was a light and fluffy pop song, but a chance for EXO-Ls to hear more of Xiumin than they had previously. It also had a fun and innocently flirty video in which we saw a fair-haired Xiumin as the sweetest boy next door. The result of another fun collaboration was released in July 2016, when Xiumin teamed up with Mark from NCT for 'Young and Free'. Xiumin had been a mentor and friend to the young rapper ever since he was a baby trainee and the chemistry is evident in the rap versus vocal duet.

Xiumin might not have had as many opportunities to display his acting talents as some of his bandmates – but when he has, he has made a mark. In 2015, he played the co-lead in the romantic drama *Falling for Challenge*, which was the most-watched web drama in South Korea that year. He made his movie debut a year later in the costume drama *Seondal: The Man Who Sells the River*, in which his fellow actors congratulated him on his acting skills and attitude. In 2018, he was also a natural selection for a new variety show called *It's Dangerous Beyond the Blankets*, in which home-loving celebrities go on a trip together. He became a very popular member of the cast, with EXO-Ls particularly loving the swimming-pool episode featuring an abs-tastic Xiumin.

Looking back at the shy, baby-faced boy who made his debut, it's hard to believe he has grown into the ripped and rugged star who can hold a whole stadium of fans in the palm of his hand. He's still a private person, but says that now, having shared so many memories over the years, he is so much closer to EXO-Ls. Fans, of course, love him whatever. He's their *yojeong* (fairy) and he always will be.

SEVEN

SUCCESS AND SHOCK

'We will remember this exact time: Friday 22 November 2013 at forty-three minutes and forty-four seconds past eleven. We will never forget this time and we will always work hard. Thank you so much.' So said Suho, accepting the *daesang* for Album of the Year at the MAMAs.

A *daesang* – the main prize at a major award ceremony – is the ultimate accolade afforded to a K-pop act. In the West, only a Grammy carries anything like the same weight and kudos. From H.O.T. to Shinhwa to BIGBANG, every great act was confirmed through their *daesangs*. For EXO to receive such an honour less than two years since debut was incredible. Indeed, they were the first of their generation (groups who debuted after 2010) to achieve the feat.

> For EXO to receive a *daesang* less than two years since debut was incredible.

A week earlier 'Growl' had earned EXO their first Song of the Year *daesang* at the MMAs and, as the awards season got under way, it was clear that the group were going to be major players at every ceremony. However, they were still not finished with 2013. At the end of November, SM revealed that EXO had a surprise Christmas present for fans: a new EP!

After the customary teasing, new music videos, in Korean and Mandarin versions, were posted on YouTube for 'Miracles in December', the lead track on the special festive EP. The EXO logo was transformed again, this time into a snowflake, and in a light-hearted photoshoot the members were dressed identically in green shirts with red bow ties, hats and braces, blue jeans and boots. They were Santa's most handsome little helpers ever.

'Miracles in December' remains a tear-jerking favourite, a delicate ballad sung to a simple piano accompaniment with flourishes from the strings. The heartfelt lyrics tell of a desire to recapture a lost love, but it is the beautiful vocals – Baekhyun and Chen on both versions with D.O. on the EXO-K track and Luhan on the EXO-M version – that tug at the heartstrings and take the song to a higher level, both in terms of the solos and the harmonies.

In the video, which features the whole group, the boys venture out into a perfect Christmas scene dressed in their smart winter clothes and carrying their presents. Their superpowers are also referenced as Xiumin completes the romantic setting by making it snow and Tao turns back time in an attempt to find that lost love again. As the song closes, tears well up in all their eyes – revealing that their efforts at reconciliation have been in vain.

The rest of the group were highlighted in the other tracks on the EP, which included slow 90s-style R&B songs in 'Christmas Day' and 'Turn to Cry'; an up-tempo, soft-rap track in 'The Star'; and a more traditional K-pop-style festive number in 'The First Snow', another song of lost love with a sweet refrain of 'Merry, Merry Christmas'. K-pop enthusiasts were used to entertainment companies releasing holiday-themed singles, but the EXO fandom soon realized that this was no hastily put-together cash-in on the success of 'Growl', but a carefully crafted collection of quality music.

In mid-December, the group promoted the EP on YouTube by hosting their own fake radio show in five five-minute episodes. Titled *Oven Radio* (a play on the words *oh-beun*, which together mean 'five minutes' in Korean), it featured a different track each day and different combinations of members. They talked about subjects related to the release and had some fun, including remembering their first impressions of each other, singing carols, and having a freestyle rap battle and a try-to-cry competition.

Once again, EXO – with Baekhyun, Chen and D.O. performing – promoted 'Miracles in December' on the TV music shows before the EP was released. In future shows they were joined by Luhan and Lay, and eventually all twelve members appeared. In the process, they racked up nine more music-show wins, including a triple crown on *M Countdown*, and were denied more only because some shows didn't have a competition on their Christmas specials. On release, the single was an immediate 'all-kill' (first place on all the principle digital charts) and the EXO-K EP went to number one in South Korea, with the EXO-M version at number two!

SM had lined up a real Christmas treat for home fans with a week of special festive performances from their top groups. SHINee, Girls' Generation, Super Junior and TVXQ all featured, but the evenings of Christmas Eve and Christmas Day saw f(x) and EXO play a joint concert. EXO's set consisted of over a dozen songs, including those on the *Miracles* EP, before they joined forces with f(x) for some festive jollity, including Chen duetting with Luna from f(x) on 'Have Yourself a Merry Little Christmas' and the groups combining for the seasonal classics 'Magic Castle' and 'Jingle Bell Rock'.

But there was still time for one more achievement in this astonishing year, and as 2013 drew to a close it was announced that physical sales of *XOXO* had reached 1 million copies. As the first K-pop act to hit this milestone for more than twelve years, many observers gave the group credit for almost singlehandedly reviving the Korean physical-format music market.

As 2013 drew to a close it was announced that physical sales of *XOXO* had reached 1 million copies.

K-pop fans can be dismissive of the success of groups that they don't personally stan, and many say the MAMA and MMA awards are aimed at international fans and are weighted towards idol groups. The real test, they say, comes in the New Year ceremonies, so a lot of humble pie was eaten when EXO collected two more *daesangs* at the Golden Disc Awards and the Seoul Music Awards. That brought the total to four – more than most groups earn in their whole careers.

With their profile established, some of the members now found themselves taking up opportunities outside the group. Baekhyun and Suho embarked on an ongoing role as joint MCs on the *Inkigayo* music show and the leader also had an acting role in three episodes of a TV drama called *Prime Minister and I*. Chanyeol went to the islands of Micronesia and joined the cast of the TV survival series *Law of the Jungle*, while Luhan, Xiumin and Tao competed in the *Idol Star Athletics Championships* – the annual sporting event for K-pop stars.

Meanwhile, Chen had joined other selected SM artists for a project called SM The Ballad. This ad-hoc group, specifically formed to sing ballads, released a mini-album in February 2014 called *Breath*. Chen appeared on two of the six tracks on the Korean version, duetting with SHINee vocalist Jonghyun and Krystal from Girls' Generation. On the Chinese version he sang the title track alongside the female Chinese singer Zhang Liyin. On release, Chen promoted the tracks on Korean music shows and joined the others for fan signings.

Seoul Fashion Week in March saw them all back together wearing outfits in the varying textures and shades of black of trendy designer Byungmun Seo. The boys walked the runway like natural-born models and performed 'Growl' at the prestigious show's grand ceremony. EXO's own fashion venture, Stardium, was also part of Fashion Week with a mini-collection featuring EXO T-shirts, reminiscent of football shirts, each printed with a member's date of birth, in white (for EXO-K) or grey (for EXO-M).

Then the rumours started. Fuelled by fan photos of various members sporting new blond locks, an imminent comeback was predicted. As excitement built, an SM missive on 1 April 2014 (of all days!) confirmed

Then the rumours started. Fuelled by fan photos of various members sporting new blond locks, an imminent comeback was predicted.

the speculation: an EP called *Overdose* would drop on 21 April. The exquisite teaser photos did indeed feature a blond Suho, Kai and Tao (Xiumin's pink pixie cut also attracted attention), with all the members in elegant and stylish buttoned-up white shirts.

The showcase was performed live to 8,000 fans at the Jamsil Indoor Stadium in Seoul on 15 April. As they were due to promote the comeback separately in Korea and China it was to be the last chance for a while to see all twelve members together and excitement was at fever pitch. As the boys took to the stage to play 'Wolf' and 'Growl', some fans were injured in the crush to get near their idols. Kai pleaded with them to be careful, and eventually they settled down to hear excerpts from the new tracks and full versions of 'Run' and 'Overdose', and to see the first showing of the new music video. With the whole event, including the Q&A session, streamed live, it was clear that the new EP was going to go big, and EXO still had a week of promotions on music shows before release to ramp up the excitement even further.

However, the very next morning, South Korea and the rest of the world woke up to news of a tragedy. MV *Sewol*, a ferry heading from the Korean mainland to the holiday island of Jeju, had sunk. More than 300 passengers and crew died in the disaster – many of them teenagers from the same South Korean school. As the rescue operation continued and many South Koreans joined the yellow-ribbon mourning campaign, the country was in no mood for pop music and SM made the sensitive decision to postpone the EXO release.

It was a difficult time for many fans, who were impatient for the comeback but deeply upset about the tragedy. In this time alone the 'Overdose' teaser amassed 5 million views and the pre-orders set a record for a mini-album by breaking the 600,000 mark. Meanwhile, fans of EXO and other groups organized care packages for the families of those affected by the Sewol ferry disaster, who were still gathered near where the boat had sunk.

The fans' wait finally ended on 7 May 2014 when the five-track EP was dropped and the video for 'Overdose' released. The music video, in Korean and Mandarin versions, featured more one-shot takes, topped and tailed with dramatic trapped-in-a-labyrinth scenes. While it was a shot-in-a-box-style video with a monochrome maze pattern background, the choreography, zooming camera movement and close-ups provided more than enough excitement. The boys looked great in colourful, baggy hip-hop gear in some scenes and in sharp suits – some even all-white – in others.

The dance, which utilized all the members, together and separately, bristled with urgency, energy and power. It was clearly as enjoyable to perform as it was to watch. 'EXO-K members had to run around trying to hide while the EXO-M members were being filmed,' revealed Chanyeol, 'so we didn't get caught by the camera. It was fun!' The lightning-paced, sharply synchronized moves were all there, but there were also so many great details to notice, among them the skipping-rope dance, the tap on the wrist at the 'Call the doctor' line, the head-drumming and cheek-popping, members grabbing and directing the camera and, out of nowhere, an amazing light flash thrown from Chen to Lay.

The track itself, a collaboration between US hitmakers The Underdogs (who had worked with Beyoncé, Britney Spears and on Girls' Generation's 'Mr.Mr.') and Korean songwriters, was a driving urban dance track with a hip-hop feel, R&B hooks and electronic beats. Its simple lyrics played on the idea of love as an addiction, with – for the first time in an EXO song – some great English lines woven in.

In under ten hours, the K and M versions combined had accumulated a million views on YouTube. The EP was also going stratospheric with songs that seem designed to showcase the group's vocal abilities, especially on the ballad 'Moonlight' and the smooth 'Thunder', while

'Overdose' was an immediate all-kill, topping the Korean digital ratings, and the rest of both the EXO-K and EXO-M EP tracks lined up behind it, dominating the charts.

the infectious pop and up-tempo rhythm of 'Run' perfectly complemented the lead track. 'Overdose' was an immediate all-kill, topping the Korean digital ratings, and the rest of both the EXO-K and EXO-M EP tracks lined up behind it, dominating the charts.

On 11 May, the whole group took the comeback showcase to China where 10,000 fans packed the Mercedes-Benz Arena in Shanghai, but once again SM divided the groups and gave them separate promotional schedules. EXO-M took the first honours, winning CCTV's *Global Chinese Music Chart*, China's first Korean-style music-competition show. Then, days later, as the Korean music shows began broadcasting again after the ferry disaster, EXO-K took the *Show Champion* trophy, beginning a run of eight victories that included a triple crown on *Inkigayo*.

Overdose had also made a huge splash internationally; the Korean version topped iTunes charts across Asia and figured highly as far afield as Brunei, Panama, Scandinavia, Mexico and Peru. In the US, it broke into the iTunes Top 100 at number sixty-five, reached second place in the *Billboard* World Albums Chart and 129 on the *Billboard* 200. Simultaneously, EXO-M saw their version place in the iTunes Top 100 in thirteen countries, including breaking the top ten in Thailand, Singapore, Malaysia and Indonesia. It was just the momentum they needed as the whole group were about to embark on a tour taking in many major cities all across Asia.

This was due to begin on 24 and 25 May 2014 at the Seoul Olympic Stadium with EXO's first solo concert, which was titled 'EXO #1: The Lost Planet in Seoul'. Tickets had gone on sale on 16 April with all 42,000 seats selling out in just 1.47 seconds. However, as excitement built, there was a massive shock in store for EXO fans, who now numbered in the millions.

On 15 May 2014, Kris issued a lawsuit demanding the termination of his contract with SM, claiming the contract violated his basic human rights. The leader of EXO-M had left the group and the fallout was massive. Fans stormed Twitter, Instagram and Facebook demanding SM and the rest of the group persuade him to stay, while much was made of EXO members unfollowing Kris's Instagram account and some enigmatic tweets that some interpreted as questioning Kris's actions. That same day, when collecting the *M Countdown* trophy, Suho said, 'I sincerely love the EXO members. Our motto is "We are one" and like the motto says we'll become an EXO that think about EXO and our fans instead of just our individual selves.' One thing was for sure: with just a week to prepare for the biggest live show of their careers, EXO were now down to eleven men.

LAY

FACT FILE

Name: Zhang Yixing

Stage name: Lay/Lay Zhang

Date of birth: 7 October 1991

Birthplace: Changsha, China

Nationality: Chinese

Height: 1.79 metres (5'10")

Position in EXO: dancer, vocalist

Sub-unit(s): EXO-M

EXO superpower: healing

EIGHT

LAY

I n every country visited by EXO on their EXO'luXion tour, chants of 'Zhang Yixing' would ring around the auditorium. He wasn't even there, and many feared he had left the group forever, but they loved him anyway. However, their dimpled unicorn had made a promise that he would never leave and his participation in 2018's 'Tempo' proved he was determined to keep his word.

Since August 2015, Lay has been the only Chinese member of the group and his participation in EXO's shows has become increasingly sporadic. Some of this has been due to strained political relations between South Korea and China, but much is down to SM giving Lay the freedom to build his career in his home country. And he's certainly succeeded at that: he is now a household name in China, ranked among the nation's top twenty celebrities, and has around 30 million followers on Weibo (the Chinese equivalent of Twitter).

Zhang Yixing was something of a star before he even joined EXO, and has been singing, dancing and acting since he was a small boy. At the age of six he had a starring role in the 1998 Chinese television drama *We the People* and, as a result, appeared on a number of variety shows and became quite

> Zhang Yixing was something of a star before he even joined EXO, and has been singing, dancing and acting since he was a small boy.

a celebrity in his home town of Changsha, a city in Hunan province in the heart of China.

Yixing is an only child who has always expressed his love for his parents (especially his mother) and his maternal grandparents, who lived with the family when he was growing up. He even dedicated his 2017 single 'I Need U' to his grandparents on their fiftieth wedding anniversary. His father, a keen folk singer, and his Michael Jackson-loving mother nurtured his love of performance and music, and by ten he was thrilling the family with his own Michael Jackson impersonations.

In 2005 he entered *Star Academy*, a talent show on Hunan TV. He came third in the competition, but made a strong impression on viewers. A Zhang Yixing fan club, XingPark, was formed and is still going strong today, making it easily EXO's longest-running fan base. By his mid-teens, Yixing was playing piano and guitar, writing songs and trying out some hip-hop moves, and by May 2008 he felt confident enough to travel to the neighbouring city of Wuhan to attend an SM global casting event. He was an extremely talented performer, so it wasn't a total surprise that he soon found himself packing his bags for Seoul.

Yixing was sixteen years old and alone in a foreign country. Although he had the support and structure of his management company, his early years at SM were not easy. Twice he was sent home, once because of visa problems and then more seriously for getting in a fight with another trainee (an incident he now deeply regrets). He waited anxiously for a chance to return and, when he was finally invited back, he was determined to work even harder.

Hard work became Yixing's mantra (his Weibo username translates as 'Work hard, work hard, work even harder') and he would spend hours practising, even when SM's own training schedule had ended. He even strapped sandbags to his waist so his dancing would have more power, an approach that caused him to suffer pain and injury a few years later.

His attitude and talent were noted by SM management. In 2010, SHINee, one of the jewels in SM's crown, embarked on their first world tour. Before their performance in Tokyo, vocalist Jonghyun suffered an injury that prevented him from dancing. They needed a stand-in dancer and SM turned to Yixing. It was his first taste of the big time and it made him even more determined to succeed.

Within a year he was preparing for debut along with fellow Chinese trainees Luhan, Kris and Tao. He had bonded with Kris as they had both joined SM earlier than the others, but he would soon build up a good friendship with Luhan too. SM assigned him to EXO-M (he was rumoured to have been the original leader) and gave him the name Lay, inspired by the quiet and musically talented character Hua Ze Lei in the popular Chinese drama *Meteor Garden* (based on the Korean television show *Boys Over Flowers*, which is itself based on a Japanese manga series). Yixing thought it odd (but also quite apt) as the word *lei* means 'tired' in Mandarin. Within the EXO story, Lay was given the superpower of healing, with a unicorn as his symbol – hence the first nickname given to him by fans: the 'Healing Unicorn'.

Lay was presented to fans in teaser number ten. His hair was dark with a side parting and a long fringe, he had a leopard-print shirt under a sparkling jacket, and red trousers, and his dancing was super-sexy. For many of those watching he was an instant bias, but it was later revealed that at the time he lacked confidence, feeling that his dancing and singing were okay, but that he couldn't be compared to Kai or Chen.

However, he soon became very popular, especially as his personality emerged. He came across as extremely respectful and caring, but also capable of being silly and very funny. The other members revealed how he would cook for them all and that he was a very tactile

> Lay was presented to fans in teaser number ten. His hair was dark with a side parting and a long fringe, he had a leopard-print shirt under a sparkling jacket, and red trousers, and his dancing was super-sexy.

person who was always patting the others. He was easy to love – he came out with quotes such as 'I don't date ugly girls, because I believe they don't exist' – and built up such a great relationship with fans that another dedicated group was formed. They called themselves Xingmi and he and they originally came up with the 'L' hand sign. When it was appropriated for EXO-L, he wrote a touching and generous message on Weibo, but you could tell he was a little sad to lose it.

Meanwhile, he was also demonstrating his talent in EXO's recordings and performances. As a dancer, his fluid style stood out on stage, particularly on tracks such as 'Tell Me What Is Love', 'My Lady' and 'Exodus'. His duets with Kai, especially 'Two Moons', were sensational, with Lay's street-dance moves creating a contrast to his dance partner's classic style. Although he was modest about his singing abilities, fans quickly picked up on his soft tones, which seem to carry such emotion. This was especially evident in the Chinese versions of 'For Life', 'Love Me Right' and 'Promise', and the short acoustic version of his SM Station single 'Monodrama' performed during the EXO'rDIUM shows.

When Kris and then the other Chinese members left EXO-M it hit Lay hard. Not only did everyone suspect he was also planning to go, but he felt responsible for keeping EXO-M afloat – justifying SM's faith in working with Chinese artists. He helped write the song 'Promise' and was clearly sincere in his vows to EXO-L. He even played the instrumental at a showcase in China for his second solo album in October 2017.

Lay would not leave EXO. However, the lack of opportunities to promote with EXO-M meant he increasingly sought to develop his career in his home country. In 2015, his desire to be a songwriter was supported by his company when SM set him up with his own studio in China, and his profile there was furthered by his starring role in the popular variety show *Go Fighting*.

His acting career was rejuvenated and he was soon being acclaimed for roles in TV dramas and movies. On TV he starred as an aspiring chef in *To Be a Better Man* and as an opera singer in *The Mystic Nine* (a record-breaking series that has now accumulated over 12 billion online views), while on the big screen Yixing has proved even more versatile, appearing in comedies such as *Oh My God*, *Kung Fu Yoga* and the historical drama *The Founding of an Army*.

Yixing had been writing songs as a teenager, and in 2014 he wrote and performed 'I'm Lay' and was a major contributor to 'Promise', but songwriting opportunities were relatively rare. However, in May 2016, through SM Entertainment's Station project, he released 'Monodrama' as a solo song and performed an excerpt in the acoustic section of the EXO'rDIUM shows. The song was a massive success across East Asia and in the USA, while at home it broke records by staying at number one on the Chinese VChart for five consecutive weeks.

Since 2016, Lay's appearances with EXO have grown increasingly infrequent and by the end of 2017 many assumed he would never be part of the group again, but his profile in China has grown and grown. His autobiography, titled *Standing Firm at 24*, became a bestseller, he was appointed as a publicity ambassador by the Communist Youth League of China and he has a wax statue in Madame Tussauds in Beijing and Shanghai. He has also supported a host of charitable concerns and has donated large sums to many welfare projects.

Lay's solo recording career has gone from strength to strength as well. In October 2016 he released a six-track solo mini-album entitled *Lose Control*. He produced and wrote the lyrics (and translated them himself into English, Korean and Japanese) for all the songs, including the title track, which was a number one hit in China. A year later, he followed it with a full self-penned album, *Lay 02 Sheep*. This was a million-seller in China and reached number four in the *Billboard* World Albums Chart.

> Lay's solo recording career has gone from strength to strength. In October 2016 he released a six-track solo mini-album entitled *Lose Control*.

The EDM hip-hop single 'Sheep' contained plenty of English language

LAY – 'Goodbye Christmas'

In December 2017 Lay took a leaf out of the EXO book and released his *Winter Special Gift* EP. Lay himself composed all the tracks, including the lead, which is a touching ballad about a former lover whose memory continues to haunt him. It shows Lay as the complete performer – a dancer, singer and musician – although we would have to wait for 'Sheep' to see him as a rapper. The single reached number two in China but remains a gem that is overlooked by many EXO fans.

lyrics and in August 2018 he appeared at the annual Lollapalooza music festival in Chicago, his first-ever solo stage in the US. There he debuted a remake of 'Sheep', a collaboration with hit DJ and producer Alan Walker that was many US music fans' first introduction to his music. Those who liked what they heard were delighted to discover his next album, *Namanana*, which was released in October 2018 under the name Lay and featured eleven tracks, each of them composed by Lay and recorded in Mandarin and English. Within twenty-four hours of its release, it topped iTunes charts in sixteen countries, from Mongolia to Columbia.

In the US he promoted it with a free concert in New York and appearances on breakfast TV shows. *Namanana* debuted at number twenty-one on the *Billboard* 200 Album Chart and Lay became the first Chinese artist to chart in the top ten on iTunes world charts. His profile in America was raised even further with news that he joined up with Jason Derulo and K-pop group NCT 127 for the project 'Let's Shut Up and Dance', a tribute to the late Michael Jackson. The single – due for release in 2019 – is a fitting opportunity for Lay to acknowledge his debt to the man who first inspired him.

It was great to see Lay having success on the world stage, but EXO-Ls were desperate to see him reunited with the group. The members had mentioned in interviews that they were in regular contact with Lay and he was seen attending an EXO-CBX sub-unit concert, but there was uncontained joy when SM confirmed that he would feature on the Chinese recording of and video for 'Tempo'. It marked his first return to the group in over a year, but to many it was as if he had never been away. Lay clearly felt that too. 'I love my guys,' he told *Billboard*. 'I love my members, for sure. And I just want to tell them, if you guys need me, I'll always be there.'

It was great to see Lay having success on the world stage, but EXO-Ls were desperate to see him reunited with the group.

NINE

THE LOST PLANET

Friday 23 May 2014 was another milestone in EXO's short career. That afternoon the group took to the stage in front of 14,000 fans at the Olympic Stadium in Seoul for the first of three dates (the third was added after the first two sold out immediately). It seemed pretty incredible that they were there at all. Shaken and upset by Kris's departure, the remaining eleven had had just a week to re-fashion and re-learn choreography originally devised for twelve.

Group leader Suho explained how Kris leaving affected the group. 'At that moment the biggest feeling was confusion,' he said. 'Because the concert was so close, it was psychologically and physically very difficult and painful.' Chanyeol added, 'Our biggest concern was about putting on a high-quality, perfect performance for our fans. We united as a whole and used that energy to put in extensive hours of practice and rehearsals to make a perfect performance.'

Despite these issues, the show was spellbinding, with a magnificent laser-light show and quality video backdrops. They were on stage for more than two hours, starting with

> The show was spellbinding, with a magnificent laser-light show and quality video backdrops. They were on stage for more than two hours, treating the crowd to over thirty fan favourites from *Mama*, *XOXO* and *Overdose*.

a defiant *haka* (a Māori life-celebration dance) before treating the crowd to over thirty fan favourites from *Mama*, *XOXO* and *Overdose*, featuring a combination of group and solo performances. Special treats included Lay's self-penned 'I'm Lay', Baekhyun sitting at the piano to sing 'My Turn to Cry', Luhan in a red leather jacket and abs-revealing vest driving the crowd crazy during his solo in 'The Star' and Chanyeol demonstrating his talents with a drum solo in 'Delight'.

Within a week, EXO were taking the show around Asia on their first solo tour, EXO from Exoplanet #1 The Lost Planet – first stop, two nights in Hong Kong. Through the summer, the tour then took them to eight cities in China, Taiwan, Singapore, Indonesia and Thailand. Everywhere they went, EXO played to sell-out arenas and packed concert halls. In each venue they bonded with the adoring fans. Tao would ask for the lights to be turned off so that he could take pictures of the fans and their light sticks; Suho would chat about the host city or country; and in Beijing they celebrated Chen's birthday together on stage. Although the set list was broadly similar to that first night in Seoul, every concert had its highlights.

One particular part of the show was popular wherever they went. This was where the boys picked a fan from the audience, brought her on stage and serenaded and danced around her to covers of their favourite SM songs, including Super Junior's 'Sorry Sorry', SHINee's 'Dream Girls' and 'Ring Ding Dong', and Girls' Generation's 'Tell Me Your Wish' and 'Gee'. Fan reactions online consistently suggested that they loved the moment but were all very envious!

Meanwhile, as the boys flew home between shows, EXO life went on. In June and July, Baekhyun played the lead role in the musical *Singin' In The Rain* in Seoul; D.O. took a main part in a TV drama called *It's Okay, That's Love* (Chen's solo soundtrack song for this, 'Best of Luck', topped the charts in late July); and there were the usual music shows and fan signings. They also returned to *Happy Camp*, the Chinese variety show where they seemed particularly at home.

If you're going to watch one early variety show on YouTube, make it the 5 July 2014 episode of *Happy Camp*. In a ninety-minute programme, the boys' personalities shine through as they play games and generally fool around, but this is also the first viewing of their shared dorm (like many K-pop groups, they continued to share bedrooms in the same apartment even after debut and stardom). It's a whirlwind tour, but you can still take in Chen's teddy bears, Xiumin's shoe closet ('Just like his personality, it's very well organized' says Chen), and Suho and Sehun's collection of comic books and Iron Man figures.

The most fascinating part, however, is saved for last. Individually the boys are filmed giving their innermost thoughts on being in the group, winning the *daesang*, celebrating birthdays and how they have been affected by Kris's departure. It's clear that they are deeply upset, but they also reaffirm their dedication to their fellow members. When the show returns to the studio, many of the audience are sobbing and the boys, lost in their thoughts, slowly give way to tears.

However, EXO's rocky 2014 wasn't over yet. For months, rumours had been circulating that Baekhyun was dating Taeyeon, a member of

EXO's rocky 2014 wasn't over yet. For months, rumours had been circulating that Baekhyun was dating Taeyeon, a member of Girls' Generation, and in July pictures of the couple published online seemed to confirm the relationship.

Girls' Generation, and in July pictures of the couple published online seemed to confirm the relationship. This was problematic. It wasn't that K-pop stars couldn't date. Most entertainment companies no longer include 'no dating' clauses in contracts, but artists are advised to conduct such affairs in complete secrecy. This is largely due to the intense relationship between idols and their fandom, and the way that fans' emotions can sometimes be magnified even further by social media.

On 19 June, an SM statement admitted that the two had indeed begun a relationship, having become close when the more experienced Taeyeon had acted as a mentor to Baekhyun at SM. Some fans were genuinely pleased for them, recalling the EXO member naming Taeyeon as his favourite in variety shows. Others, however, felt betrayed. They claimed that it wasn't that they couldn't bear sharing him, but that they were upset that the couple had adopted the playful couple-name 'Taengkoong', which had originally been coined by fans who had believed they were just friends; that Baekhyun had sent fans love messages that were actually intended for Taeyeon; and anyway, they said, hadn't he promised he wouldn't date until he was in his thirties?!

Within days both Baekhyun and Taeyeon took to Instagram to apologize to fans for any misunderstandings that had caused upset. Baekhyun's note read: 'I wish that our fans will no longer hurt… I will do my best to slowly approach all of you again… And EXO is a name that is so precious to me. I want to tell you that I've never thought of EXO lightly.' Although the furore died down, Baekhyun and Taeyeon's on-and-off relationship (and the bitterness of some fans) would continue into the future.

It was time for some good news and SM came up trumps. August saw the announcement of a global fan club and an official fan name: EXO-L. Although many had taken to the Exotics moniker, the word had been chosen by international fans, didn't mean anything to Koreans and had no association with the group – whereas EXO-L, it was explained, brought EXO-K and EXO-M together and, handily, also signified 'EXO Love'.

Having an official fan club was yet another landmark on EXO's journey to superstar status. Their rise had not been without its difficulties – the post-debut hiatus, the leaked 'Wolf' track, the exit of Kris, the dating scandal – but they were now established as one of SM's top acts. At the SM Town Live concert in front of 35,000 people at the Seoul World Cup stadium in August 2014 they were among the headliners, and the Lost Planet tour was continuing to play to packed and enthusiastic arenas throughout Asia.

In September, EXO were due to return to China for the final concert of the first leg of the tour. EXO-M were very popular in China, especially the Chinese members, although some fans grumbled that they lacked the backing that SM were giving to EXO-K. Luhan was perhaps the most popular member of EXO-M, inside and outside China. He had been absent from the EXO line-up at the Lost Planet concert in Bangkok in mid-September, saying he was very over-tired and suffering from headaches and dizziness, but there was no way he was going to miss the two concerts a week later in Beijing, his hometown. Indeed, he really gave it his all on stage, although in hindsight some fans read more into his tears, and Lay and Xiumin's hugs, because it was to be his last-ever performance with the group.

Luhan was absent again when EXO travelled with SM Town Live to Tokyo at the beginning of October and, just when fans were wondering whether he was ill again, on 10 October the news broke that he had taken steps to nullify his contract with SM and had left EXO. This time, the reaction from the group was sympathetic. Members seemed to understand his position and wished him well. Lay, who seemed closest to Luhan, posted on Weibo: 'Brother, goodbye! If we have the chance let's stand on stage together again. As brothers, I support your every decision. Good luck.'

Just when fans were wondering whether Luhan was ill again, on 10 October the news broke that he had taken steps to nullify his contract with SM and had left EXO.

Ironically, there was one reality in which Luhan was still part of the group. A TV series called *EXO90: 2014* had been running on Mnet since August and an episode featuring the now ex-EXO member remained to be screened. The series, which also featured a number of SM rookies (now members of idol group NCT), saw EXO meet K-pop idols from the 1990s and re-make videos of their hit songs. It was a fun idea and, with each of the group getting to star in a video, gave them a chance to show off their acting skills. It depends on your bias, but Suho's 'Dear Mom' (originally by g.o.d), Baekhyun's 'Dance With DOC' (by DJ DOC) and D.O.'s comedy turn to S.E.S.'s 'I'm Your Girl' are all worth watching, while tellingly Luhan signs off with his version of Kim Minkyo's 'The Last Game'. It's almost as if he knew…

Though EXO were down to ten men, they still had an important leg of their Lost Planet tour to complete in Japan. Making an impression there was important to EXO. The fans attending were the biggest buyers of physical CDs in the world and, despite the traditional rivalry and even hostility that existed between the two countries, Japan was developing a growing appetite for K-pop.

Back in April, EXO had introduced themselves to their Japanese fans with a series of five short performances followed by a Q&A session. It had been a resounding success, attracting more than 100,000 fans over the series. Now they were taking their solo concert there, with three nights in both Fukuoka and Tokyo in November. That they were gaining a foothold in the country was confirmed when *Overdose* was announced as the best-selling K-pop album of the year in Japan.

If EXO-Ls were still lamenting the loss of Luhan, SM were ploughing ahead as if nothing had changed. Just like the previous year, fans were

Special Stage 'Sabor a Mi' in Mexico

The South Korean TV show *Music Bank* was at the forefront of the Korean Wave, showcasing K-pop acts in countries as far away as France, Turkey and Brazil, and EXO were one of the acts that took part in a show in Mexico in late October 2014. Earlier they had performed 'Growl', but Suho, Baekhyun, D.O. and Chanyeol (with guitar) returned to play this classic by Mexican composer and singer Álvaro Carrillo – and it went viral all over South America.

to be treated to a Christmas present in the form of a brand-new release. The short teaser for 'December 2014 (The Winter's Tale)' was released on 15 December and showed Chanyeol seated at his keyboards, amusing himself with a game on his phone, as a slow and soulful intro played. It transpired that the single would be released through the app game Superstar SMTOWN four days later.

While EXO-Ls were working out that 'The Winter's Tale' was based on US artist K Michelle's 'Long Time, No See', SM announced the release of a whole new album featuring live recordings from the concerts in Seoul in May. Entitled *Exology Chapter 1: The Lost Planet*, it included thirty-six songs that captured the magic of the live performances, from the *haka* to the solo performances to the hit-filled encore. An added bonus was a set of re-worked studio versions of 'Black Pearl', 'Love, Love, Love', 'Wolf' and 'Growl' – these were special arrangements that had been devised for the live shows – and the new Christmas single. Those buying the special CD package were also treated to postcards of each member, a seventy-two-page photobook full of pictures from the live shows and a world-tour map.

'The Winter's Tale' slipped under the radar for many casual EXO-Ls as it was mainly used to promote SM's app game, but it has some beautiful vocal harmonies from D.O., Chen and Baekhyun (who seem to be a specialist festive sub-unit) and packs in the Christmas references. The song wasn't promoted on the music shows, but, proving the loss of Luhan hadn't affected EXO's popularity, it still managed to clock up a win in the first *Music Bank* show of the new year.

Trophy collecting was becoming a hobby. In early December at the MAMAs, EXO picked up two of the three *daesangs* – Album of the Year for *Overdose* and Artist of the Year. They followed it in the new year with more *daesangs* at the Golden Disc Awards and the Seoul Music Awards. It had been a year in which they had lost another member and had seen scandal hit the group, but EXO had showed incredible resilience and had been supported through thick and thin by the most dedicated of fans. They had revealed the personalities and talent behind the gorgeous glossy photos, won new fans at home and had wowed audiences across Asia with an unmatchable live show. EXO-Ls just couldn't wait to see what the future had in store.

BAEKHYUN

FACT FILE

Name: Byun Baek-hyun

Stage name: Baekhyun

Date of birth: 6 May 1992

Birthplace: Bucheon, South Korea

Nationality: South Korean

Height: 1.74 metres (5'9")

Position in EXO: vocalist

Sub-unit(s): EXO-K, EXO-CBX

EXO superpower: light

TEN

BAEKHYUN

Being a trainee is a long and gruelling process. It takes most trainees years before they are ready to debut. Unless you're a super-talented, fast learner – a natural. It took Baekhyun a mere four months' training before he was selected for EXO and a further seven months to train for their debut.

Born Byun Baek-hyun in Bucheon, a satellite city of Seoul, the future EXO singer always wanted to be a performer. 'When I was eleven years old I told my parents that I didn't think I would be able to just sit in an office because I'm very lively and I cannot stay still,' Baekhyun told *Elle Korea*. Inspired by K-pop superstar Rain, he became a singer. YouTube has a number of videos of Baekhyun with a pudding-basin haircut performing in talent shows during his school years, including singing with his band Honsusangtae (which translates as 'coma').

> YouTube has a number of videos of Baekhyun with a pudding-basin haircut performing in talent shows during his school years.

Other companies had their chance to sign the young talent. Baekhyun auditioned for many of them during his school days but received no offers. So, he sang lead vocals in his band, learned piano and prepared to go college, where he would major in music. He was twenty years old and preparing for his entrance exams when he was approached by an

SM streetcaster (agent). He thought it was a scam, but sure enough they later called and asked him to audition.

Baekhyun sang a TVXQ song at the audition. As he passed through several rounds, he picked his rival, a singer who hit the high notes with ease. Eventually they were the only two left. Despite being in competition they got on well and wished each other luck. Six months later, in 2011, SM Entertainment called Baekhyun and asked him to sign as a trainee. Just days after he started he met up again with his rival, who had also been signed. It was Chen.

Kai has recalled how peaceful the dorm was until Baekhyun and Chen showed up. The new arrivals were boisterous and noisy, and they soon found a fellow mischief-maker in Chanyeol; EXO's future beagle line (a group's extroverted and playful members) was born. When Chen was assigned to EXO-M, Baekhyun became the lead vocalist of EXO-K alongside rapper Chanyeol. The pair roomed together, so they only kept each other awake with their constant chatter!

Not that Baekhyun's good nature isn't appreciated. EXO-K members voted Baekhyun as the funniest member (Baekhyun voted for Sehun), and managers and members alike have commended him for boosting the mood of the group. He doesn't just mess around, though. As a trainee, Baekhyun had little time to get up to speed, and he worked hard at his dancing (he later thanked Kai for teaching him) and completely changed his singing style, often asking Chen for help.

Baekhyun sang on the prologue release 'What Is Love' before he was officially introduced on 30 January 2012 as EXO's ninth member. However, he remained one of the more hidden members of the group. He featured in just one teaser (number nineteen), even then appearing only briefly with a lovely fluffy white dog! Perhaps to make up for it, he was included, equally fleetingly, in Girls' Generation sub-unit TTS's music video for 'Twinkle'.

By debut, Baekhyun had been revealed as main vocalist for EXO-K. His superpower gave him the ability to manipulate light and his badge was a shining star, although new fans seemed more interested in his vocal superpowers and his ability to look drop-dead gorgeous. Baekhyun's powerful but honey-coated vocals were distinguishable in songs such as 'Angel', 'Don't Go' and 'Baby Don't Cry', and he had a look that could be smoulderingly sexy one minute and puppy-dog adorable the next.

Through his appearances on variety shows, fans were also discovering how funny Baekhyun could be. Perhaps he has such a sense of fun because he's the youngest in his family (his brother, Byun Bae-beom, is seven years his senior), but his energy and willingness to laugh at himself made him stand out. He would imitate the other members (especially poor D.O.), pull weird faces, give spoilers for the group's new choreography or come up with his own words such as the iconic *kkaebsong* (a cheeky way of saying 'what a pity'), which he first made his own on *Showtime* and which quickly made its way into fandom vocabulary.

> Baekhyun would imitate the other members, pull weird faces, give spoilers for the group's new choreography or come up with his own words such as the iconic *kkaebsong*.

He has made some legendary variety-show appearances. On *Knowing Brothers* he made the hosts blush (a rare feat indeed) with his answer to why it was Sehun's body that he was most jealous of in EXO. On *Ask Us Anything* he revealed that when he joined EXO, as one of the last members, he made sure to shower with each of the others as a bonding activity (D.O. was his favourite as he would scrub Baekhyun's back) and explained how they couldn't keep him out as he used a chopstick to pick the lock on the bathroom door! And when on *Weekly Idol* D.O. named Baekhyun last in the group's handsome ranking, Baekhyun hilariously got his revenge when listing EXO members in order of charm.

Those attending live shows get to see how much fun Baekhyun can be as he fools around and engages with audiences, but they also see his performance face – the artist who takes the business of singing very seriously indeed. As the two groups merged into one nine-man (and often, with Lay being absent, eight-man) group, Baekhyun became more and more integral to their performance. Up-tempo or ballad, his smooth and unforced mid-range vocals (with some impressive high notes too) lit up so many of the songs, with 'Lotto', 'Love Me Right', 'Drop That', 'The Eve' and, of course, 'El Dorado' among those that really brought out the best in him. His dancing rapidly improved as well. He began to be given his own solo dances in live shows and the others named Baekhyun as being the quickest to learn new choreography.

Baekhyun has also earned the title of the group's 'Eyeliner King' – a pretty hard-fought contest! – although it's not just his eyeliner but his eye make-up in general that has left EXO-Ls eagerly anticipating his look in each new concept. From the smoky eyes of 'Monster' to the red brows and liner of 'Ko Ko Bop', and from the icy frosting of 'Power' to the glittery gold highlights of 'Tempo', he slays every time. The burgundy eyeshadow he wore at the 2014 Seoul Music Awards red carpet was even credited by make-up artists as starting a major trend.

That 'Ko Ko Bop' comeback also featured Baekhyun sporting a red-streaked mullet – but if anyone could pull off this nightmare look from the 1980s, it was EXO's cherub-faced vocalist and, although it was not universally loved, he more or less did. He has pretty much rocked every hair colour: his blond (shown off to great effect in a photoshoot for *Elle Korea* in November 2015), green, rainbow, silver, violet, yellow, bright-red and flamingo-pink colourings all have their admirers, although the 2013 auburn poodle style seems to be one of his less favoured looks.

It was a particularly fetching orange that Baekhyun was sporting as EXO-CBX hit the ground running with 'Hey Mama' in October 2016. His inclusion in the sub-unit, alongside Chen and Xiumin, showed how far he had progressed. There is nowhere to hide when there are only three of you on stage, but his dancing was awesome and his singing provided the stability around which many of their songs were based. And, of course, it went without saying that he brought the fun along and was always up for doing something new. That included trying out his rap skills – and a little bit of drag. Fans had loved his appearance as 'Baekhee' (as they named her), the pretty young girl in CBX's 'The One' video, so he promised to upload a photo of 'her' if EXO-CBX won a music show. When they won first place on SBS's *The Show* he was true to his word, posting the sweet picture on his Instagram account – but only for five minutes!

Despite all the success, EXO life has not always been easy for Baekhyun. The scrutiny that celebrities come under can be difficult for someone who likes to be open about their life. In June 2014, it was revealed that he had been enjoying a secret romance with Girls' Generation's Taeyeon. The couple had known each other since Baekhyun arrived at SM Entertainment in 2011, but the relationship had only started early in 2014. The publicity, and the animosity from some fans, made it difficult for both of them and they felt it necessary to apologize for their

> Despite all the success, EXO life has not always been easy for Baekhyun. The scrutiny that celebrities come under can be difficult for someone who likes to be open about their life.

secrecy, but although there was no official announcement, the relationship seemed to come to an end sometime around the summer of 2015.

Baekhyun has had his troubles with over-obsessive fans, known as *sasaengs*, over the years. In 2013, fans turned up uninvited and caused havoc at his brother's wedding, and he has become infuriated when his V Live broadcasts have been interrupted by their incessant calls. His love for EXO-Ls runs deep, though. It was Baekhyun who invented the endearing nickname 'Aeri' for the fandom. He explained that he wanted a term that echoed the way fans called them Baekhyunnie, Minseokkie, Chennie and so on, and from the Korean pronunciation of '[EXO]L-ie' he got 'Aeri' (sometimes spelled as 'Eri'), which, wonderfully, also means 'guardian and blessing' in Korean.

Magical Circus tour 2018 – EXO-CBX – 'Ringa Ringa Ring'

EXO-CBX brought their Magical Circus to Japan in May 2018 with a full set of songs from the sub-unit, including solos from each of the guys. Creating the sub-unit gave them time and space to shine and blond Baekhyun, in oversize jacket and shirt, certainly enjoys the focus. His incredible stage presence is clear even from the video, and he takes his turn to show what he's got and gives it everything in a full-on explosion of dance, rap and some sweet vocals.

Since debut, Baekhyun has been quick to take up the other opportunities that arise when you're a K-pop star. Alongside Suho, he spent most of 2014 as the host of music show *Inkigayo*, and even found time to play the main role of Don Lockwood in the Seoul production of the musical *Singin' in the Rain* to many positive reviews. In 2016 he made his acting debut in the popular K-drama *Moon Lovers: Scarlet Heart Ryeo*. His role as Prince Wang Eun involved kissing, crying and dying scenes and Baekhyun smashed it, winning the Popularity Award (Actor) at the Asia Artist Awards.

Having always looked great in understated comfortable and cool clothes, it seemed a natural fit when, in 2018, US streetwear brand Privé invited Baekhyun to partner with them – but this was not just an endorsement deal or a modelling assignment: they wanted his creative input. Baekhyun had no design experience and had never even been to a fashion show, but he threw himself into the project. He did his own research and arrived at meetings with sketches and inspirational photographs. The result was a line of affordable street-style T-shirts, sweaters and hoodies that totally reflected the star's own style – simple and very cool.

Surprisingly, it was a full three years after debut before Baekhyun released any music outside EXO, but when he did, his stunning solo 'Beautiful', the OST to *EXO Next Door*, became the first OST single from a web drama to top the digital charts in Korea. In January 2016, Baekhyun also duetted with Suzy (who had been in girl group Miss A) in an old-fashioned, jazz-styled number called 'Dream'. It had immense charm and a warm romantic vibe, and was accompanied by a video in which Baekhyun wore suitably retro attire, but matched it with subtly pink-tinged hair and luscious pink lipstick. The song went to number one for three weeks, racked up five music-show wins and led to the duo picking up prizes at MAMA, Melon and the Golden Disc Awards.

> Baekhyun had no design experience and had never even been to a fashion show, but he threw himself into the project. He did his own research and arrived at meetings with sketches and inspirational photographs.

Other notable duets followed. In 2017, 'Rain', another beautiful slow number, which culminated in fabulous harmonies, was a hit with Soyou, a former member of girl group Sistar, and then in 2018 Baekhyun teamed up with rapper Loco in a socially aware, follow-your-dream song called 'Young', in which he was able to let rip with some expressive vocals.

In February 2018, Baekhyun gave a very special solo performance – there were no fan chants, screams or even a backing track, just a children's choir accompanying him. He had been invited to sing the national anthem at the International Olympic Committee general assembly opening ceremony in front of the South Korean president and 900 other dignitaries – not bad for someone who didn't become a trainee until he was twenty years old!

ELEVEN

WE ARE ONE

'Many of you have thought that 2014 was a black year for EXO. But from today, from this stage on MAMA onwards, the colour "black" will be redefined. You know what, I believe 2015 will be the colourful year for EXO.' Lay had spoken those optimistic words from the stage at an awards ceremony in December and, within the first month of the new year, teasers for an EXO comeback were emerging.

The first official information came in a teaser for a new live show, EXO Planet #2 – The EXO'luXion (note how SM cleverly amalgamated the group's name, 'revolution' and the 'X' for the ten remaining members). Meanwhile, EXO-Ls who had been following the group from the outset were very excited when they recognized the backing track – it was 'El Dorado', the song used in Chanyeol's pre-debut teaser.

How long did it take them to sell out the 67,000 tickets for the four dates (they would later add another) at Seoul's Olympic Gymnastics Arena in the first week of March? Just 0.4 seconds, which broke their own record, set when they'd debuted The Lost Planet in the city. In

> How long did it take them to sell out the 67,000 tickets for the four dates at Seoul's Olympic Gymnastics Arena in the first week of March? Just 0.4 seconds, which broke their own record.

the press conference, Suho revealed that a new album was imminent and that EXO would be performing all the new tracks during the set.

The concert united every aspect of EXO into a kaleidoscope of colour, energy and excitement. It continued the narrative of the boys as superhero figures from another planet arriving on Earth where their lives are threatened; it allowed them all to look their best in outfits that changed from gold lamé jackets to two-tone burgundy suits with black shirts to pink shirts and plaid trousers; it showed off their fun and charming sides; and, most of all, it provided a breathtaking light-and-video backdrop to their incredible knife-sharp choreography and musical talent.

There were so many highlights to the show. The first-ever performance of 'El Dorado' was accompanied by hip-action dancing and *Star Wars*-style lightsabers; Kai and Sehun rolled in an on-stage pool in an amazing dance to 'Baby Don't Cry'; a Christmas segment brought out the boys' playful side as they emerged dressed as elves; the group changed on stage, silhouetted behind a screen; and Chanyeol DJ'd on a turntable platform as they got the whole crowd on their feet. EXO'luXion proved that EXO were stronger than ever; despite the hardships of 2014 they had come back with style and that was just the start.

SM had never let go of EXO's mythical back story and in mid-March they set EXO-Ls a treasure hunt. Over ten days they uploaded a series of one-minute videos called 'Pathcode', each featuring an individual member in a different city, caught in a tantalizingly mysterious situation. SM also released cryptic hints on Twitter. If fans could work out the code they could access the teaser photos on the SM website. In addition, the first letters of the city names formed an anagram of EXO's next single. It certainly kept EXO-Ls busy while they waited for the comeback.

The basic story seemed to suggest that only ten of them (smart, eh?) had escaped the maze of the *Overdose* EP, and the *Exodus* album found them on Earth being tested. Chanyeol would later reveal that the hidden message of the 'Pathcode' videos was 'awakening': the members' supernatural powers had come to life and they were ready for the next stage. All this inspired plenty of theories online, but most were happy to enjoy the videos, input the codes (or look at the pictures uploaded by those who had!) and enjoy the beautiful moody black-and-white teaser photos.

'We think that through this new album you will be able to see a brighter and more evolved side of each of the members,' said Suho. The members emphasized that they saw OT10 (OT stands for 'One True' and the number indicates the number in the group at that time) as a new chapter that marked a more mature sound for the group, stressing how hard they had all worked to improve their musical abilities. Of course, the physical album – EXO having done so much to revive interest in the format – came in Korean and Chinese versions, packaged in silver and gold respectively, but each of these also came in ten different versions, offering a choice of member on the cover. Collect all ten and the spines lined up to form the new logo: a striking wireframe hexagon – or was it a 3D cube? With a fifty-two-page photobook, postcards and a poster, they really had tried to give fans something special and, as a thank you to EXO-L's, SM had quietly uploaded one song, 'First Love', for a limited period of just ten hours on 29 March.

The ten-track *Exodus* was released on 30 March. Pre-orders for the Korean and Chinese albums had already passed the half-a-million mark and the lead single, 'Call Me Baby', which had been released three days earlier, had gone straight to number five in the Korean digital charts.

'Call Me Baby' was everything they said new EXO was going to be. It had a fast-paced R&B sound full of hooks,

Pre-orders for the Korean and Chinese versions of *Exodus* had already passed the half-a-million mark and the lead single, 'Call Me Baby', which had been released three days earlier, had gone straight to number five in the Korean digital charts.

beats and brassy notes, and it was innovative in that they took a turn-of-the-millennium boyband style and updated it with rap and dance sections, a falsetto chorus and sumptuous production from iconic producer Teddy Riley (who had worked with Michael Jackson and Bobby Brown). It was assured, confident and signalled a new musical maturity.

Many still laud *Exodus* as the group's finest full album. At its heart it has a sound of its own and contains a superb balance of dance, pop and ballads. It has lyrics that resonate and utilizes the vocal range of the whole group. Among these tracks, a few have become live favourites. 'El Dorado', the song fans had waited three years for, was destined to become a classic from the moment the group sang it on the Seoul Olympic Park stage. With its Middle Eastern feel, incredible high notes from Baekhyun, infectious chant, powerful beat and lyrics about facing obstacles on the journey to success together, it is packed with power and emotion.

Other fan picks include the ballad 'My Answer', beautifully sung to a piano backing; the smooth and sultry 'Playboy' (written by SHINee vocalist Jonghyun); and 'Transformer', with its lyrics about a girl who is impossible to work out but ultimately irresistible, heavy electro-beat, rap feel and great English lines – who doesn't love D.O.'s 'Tick, tick, boom, boom, 'bout to blow'? But that doesn't mean the other tracks are filler – from the upbeat 'Exodus' to 'Beautiful', another track originally heard on a pre-debut teaser, they all help to establish a very distinctive EXO sound.

The last two music videos had made the 'one-shot' technique EXO's own and although 'Call Me Baby' is not a one-shot, as it has changes of scene and costume, it does follow that style. While some fans were disappointed that the aesthetics of the beautifully filmed teasers had not been followed, the simple movement through a series of rooms does enable the boys' looks, personality and dance skills to come to the fore. There are cheeky moments, such as when four of them unexpectedly emerge from the car, or Tao's subtle wink, and the choreography is smooth, the styling is casual – sportswear, skinny ripped black jeans

EXO 'Call Me Baby' *M Countdown* episode 418

This is EXO going public with 'Call Me Baby'. It's 2 April 2015 and their first music-show promotion for the track. There are so many reasons to dig out this video. Firstly, this is how to make a music-show promotion look like a music video, as EXO utilize the set to the max, with perfect transitions between sub-units. Secondly, they completely nail the choreography and look fabulous (it's back to black for Lay). Finally, it's the last we see of OT10. Tao is clearly struggling here with a painful ankle; he missed the rest of the promotions, and would never appear on stage with EXO again.

and leather jackets. There are also some great close-ups of Chanyeol's ashy-grey hair, with Lay as a blond and Chen's perm catching EXO-L's attention as well.

Whichever way you cut it, EXO were causing a stir. 'Call Me Baby' got to number two on the South Korean Chart (beaten to the top spot by Miss A) and hit the same position on the *Billboard* World Digital Song Sales Chart; they even broke into the Canadian Hot 100 at number ninety-eight. The videos (in Korean and Chinese) had received over 4 million views in just twenty-four hours and the music-show wins just kept coming. They won triple crowns on all five shows and even when they stopped promoting, at the end of April, they took a fourth consecutive victory on *Show Champion*, *M Countdown* and *Show! Music Core*. In all, they bagged eighteen trophies – a record for a single song.

Everything should have been perfect – except this is EXO and they seemed jinxed. Once again, the bombshell came from the West. Tao, dogged by an ankle injury he incurred when playing football in the *Idol Star Athletics Championships* in February, had returned to China to recuperate, missing almost the entire promotional period. On 22 April 2015, Tao's father posted a letter on Weibo, stating that his son had left the group due to health issues and a lack of support from the company for individual career development. Tao's own message to the fans was simple. It said: 'Sorry. Grateful.'

While the rest of the group stayed silent, the reaction from EXO-Ls was varied. Some – those who knew about his injuries – had half-expected the news, others harkened back to Tao's words when Kris left, while many just shrugged their shoulders because they were getting used to it. The question of where that left EXO-M remained up in the air. They were not, and still have not been, officially disbanded, but they would never appear again. From now on it was just EXO – they were one.

> On 22 April 2015, Tao's father posted a letter on Weibo, stating that his son had left the group due to health issues and a lack of support from the company for individual career development. Tao's own message to the fans was simple. It said: 'Sorry. Grateful.'

Fortunately, a distraction came in the story of Ji Yeon-hee, a 23-year-old woman who was a massive EXO fan. When her mother asked her to clean the house next door that she had rented out, she discovered that the new tenants were none other than Chanyeol, D.O., Baekhyun and Sehun. Of course, it was all fiction. Not fan fiction (although the plot certainly wouldn't be out of place in a fanfic), but a web drama called *EXO Next Door*, a story spread over sixteen quarter-of-an-hour episodes broadcast on Naver, a video-streaming service in Asia.

The series pulled in 50 million views, and follows Yeon-hee, played by Moon Ga-young, as she begins to get close to D.O. before she realizes that Chanyeol was her childhood crush and a tricky love triangle ensues as the rest of the group turn up at the house. EXO-Ls lapped it up, appreciating that, while it might not be Shakespeare, the series had an interesting storyline, was a lot of fun and provided a great opportunity to see more of the boys acting.

The new nine-man EXO started the summer by making a statement of intent. With 'Call Me Baby' still fresh in the public's minds, they unleashed 'Love Me Right', a fresh and springy number that had all the makings of a holiday hit. The driving baseline, horns that leaped out from the electronic track and surging synths perfectly matched the lyrics, which described the rush you feel when you're in love. Throw in a chorus that's hard to get out of your head and the song is off the feel-good scale. It is perhaps one of the most underrated tracks in the EXO catalogue, although EXO-Ls will never forget Sehun's cry of 'Shawty imma party till the sundown,' the inspiration for many a meme.

The accompanying video, uploaded on 3 June 2015, marked a departure from the usual EXO style. In a collage of colourful scenes, EXO appeared as American-football players on the field and in the locker room, as friends hanging out in a funky room and as low-level bad boys with spray cans, but these sequences were intercut with forest scenes of high angst and, of course, dancing, which took place in a futuristic warehouse with the boys wearing groovy black-and-white striped suits. For those who missed having the full dance to enjoy, SM uploaded EXO's dance-practice video at the end of July, and it's a fun and (relatively) easy one to learn.

When the nine debuted the song on *M Countdown* on 4 June they gave a straightforward, natural performance in which they just looked so happy. Due to the group's other commitments, it would be a short promotion – but no one could doubt their growing success. The track went one better than 'Call Me Baby' by hitting the top of the Korean charts (their second number one) and reaching number three on the *Billboard* World Digital Song Sales Chart. Once again, EXO did a fair job of sweeping up on the music shows with eleven more

'Love Me Right' hit the top of the Korean charts and reached number three on the *Billboard* World Digital Song Sales Chart.

wins, including yet more triple crowns on *Show Champion* and *Show! Music Core*.

Love Me Right was also the title given to a repackaged version of *Exodus*, which contained the original ten songs, the new single and three other numbers. These were high-quality tracks. 'First Love' (which had been revealed earlier as a gift to fans) was a sweet and simple R&B cut featuring vocals from all nine members, while 'Tender Love' was another great funky dance number. The final new track, 'Promise (EXO 2014)', became arguably the most meaningful song to the members and fans alike. It was the first song that the group had had a hand in writing, with Lay composing both Korean and Chinese versions of the song, and writing the Chinese lyrics, with Chen and Chanyeol writing the Korean lyrics; but, more than this, it was a passionate and personal message to fans. They apologized for breaking their promise that they would stay together, offered thanks for the support they had received and made a new promise to devote themselves to their fans in the future. It is both sad and uplifting, and is cherished by EXO-L. Now, more than ever, they knew those words were true: 'We are one'.

KRIS

FACT FILE

Name: Wu Yifan (born Li Jiaheng)

Stage name: Kris/Kris Wu

Date of birth: 6 November 1990

Birthplace: Guangzhou, China

Nationality: Chinese-Canadian

Height: 1.87 metres (6'2")

Position in EXO: leader of EXO-M, rapper, vocalist

Sub-unit(s): EXO-M

Date left EXO: May 2014

EXO superpower: flight

TWELVE

KRIS, LUHAN AND TAO

It is certainly not rare for members to leave a K-pop group, but the departures of Kris, Luhan and Tao in 2014 and 2015 came as a blow to EXO and their fans. The loss of three valued members of the group affected the morale of the remaining members and blew apart SM Entertainment's plan to operate twin groups in China and South Korea. Fans felt torn: on the one hand, they couldn't help but feel betrayed by those who had stood alongside fellow members claiming 'We are one' and then left; on the other, the affection they felt for the three didn't simply disappear. Indeed, many fans have continued to follow Kris, Luhan and Tao, and support their post-EXO careers.

Kris was the first member to leave EXO, in May 2014, as the group began to promote 'Overdose'. Kris was not only an integral member of EXO-M, but he was also the leader of the sub-group and its only fluent English speaker. His departure came as a shock to fans and certainly to the other members, who reacted with disappointment and some anger at his decision. After all, they had already been through so much together.

Wu Yifan grew up in China until he was ten, when he moved with his mother to Vancouver, Canada. The teenage Yifan was a promising basketball player who even considered playing professionally, and it was through basketball that he heard and became interested in hip-hop. In 2007, when he was eighteen, he attended an SM Entertainment global audition event in Vancouver. He knew nothing of SM or K-pop, but sang

In 2007, when Yifan was eighteen, he attended an SM Entertainment global audition event in Vancouver. He knew nothing of SM or K-pop, but sang and did a little break dancing – and the next thing he knew he was on his way to Korea to be a trainee!

and did a little break dancing – and the next thing he knew he was on his way to Korea to be a trainee!

Wu Yifan would spend four years as an SM trainee in Seoul. It was a tough time for a boy not familiar with Korean culture. He spent long hours training and felt incredibly homesick. However, he befriended American-Korean (and future music producer) Kevin Shin, slowly opened up to his co-trainees and even received some exposure on a Girls' Generation concert DVD.

He was given the name Kris, and on 16 February 2012 he appeared alone in the EXO teaser seventeen, in which he was seen jumping from the top of a building. The following day, when he was confirmed as the group's eleventh member, fans were relieved to discover that he had the superpower of flight. He was also made leader of EXO-M, a role given to him by SM because he had a caring nature and could speak Mandarin, English and Korean. He soon built a reputation for a love of fashion and, perhaps wrongly, for being a cold character. This was partly due to the reality series *Showtime* – in particular a chicken-eating challenge in episode one, which became quite a talking point for fans. In this, Kris exclaimed rather disdainfully that 'Chicken is not my style' yet five minutes later was seen tucking in. What was that about, they asked?

Kris has since explained that he left EXO for a number of reasons, including missing his family in China, the injuries and illness he suffered during his time with the group, and wanting more freedom to pursue his solo ambitions. He never rejoined EXO and his legal disputes with SM Entertainment were finally settled in July 2016.

Kris's exit from EXO coincided with a boom in the Chinese film industry and, as a high-profile celebrity, Kris Wu (as he was now known) put aside his music career to become a movie star. His debut, *Somewhere Only We Know*, was the top-ranking title at the Chinese box office in 2015 and his follow-up, *Mr Six*, became one of the highest-grossing films in China ever. His film career then went international with movies such as 2017's *XXX: Return of Xander Cage* with Vin Diesel and he kept his music career alive too, releasing hip-hop singles that reached the top ten in China. In November 2018, however, his focus returned to rapping, with a mostly English language album, *Antares*, which (just) made the *Billboard* 100 in the US.

Kris Wu is a now a major star in China and a global celebrity. He became the youngest person to have a wax figure on display at Madam Tussauds in Shanghai, has appeared as a catwalk model for Burberry in London and was made a global ambassador for the fashion brand, and has even returned to the basketball court for NBA All-Star Games. He has indicated that he no longer has any communication with the other members of EXO, but clearly values the time he spent with them and has said, 'I treasure every moment. I feel that without that I would never be able to be who I am today.'

Kris Wu is a now a major star in China and a global celebrity.

LUHAN

FACT FILE

Name: Lu Han

Stage name: Luhan

Date of birth: 20 April 1990

Birthplace: Beijing, China

Nationality: Chinese

Height: 1.78 metres (5'10")

Position in EXO: vocalist, dancer

Sub-unit(s): EXO-M

Date left EXO: October 2014

EXO superpower: telekinesis

Of the three members who have left EXO, Luhan is probably the most missed by EXO-Ls and by the group themselves. With boyish good looks, the voice of an angel and a generous and open soul, Luhan was always hard not to love and since leaving EXO he has become one of the biggest stars in China.

As a youngster, Luhan had two passions – football and music. His parents didn't think much of the idea of professional football and were only slightly less discouraging about the prospect of their son becoming a pop singer, so they were probably relieved when, in 2008, he auditioned for JYP Entertainment in China and was rejected. However, he took himself off to language school in Korea and later that year, when he was shopping in Myeong-dong in Seoul, he was picked out by an SM Entertainment streetcaster. It was 2010 when he actually signed as a trainee and there was no stopping him now. He was ultra-sociable, bonded with the other Chinese members, shared his love of football with Xiumin and developed a close relationship with Sehun.

When, on 27 December 2011, Luhan became the second EXO member to be introduced, dancing alongside Kai in the second of the teasers, fans of this new group also took an immediate liking to the tall but baby-faced member. And, when they heard him singing with Chen on EXO-M's 'Baby Don't Cry', they realized he had a voice to die for too.

With EXO-M, Luhan's popularity soared in China and internationally. It seemed he could carry off any hair colour or style – swept-back pink, tumbling red curls or messy neon orange. His vocals were one of the reasons many preferred some of EXO-M's versions of the songs, especially 'My Lady', 'Black Pearl' and 'Heart Attack', but then, on 11 October 2014, barely four months after Kris's exit, Luhan announced that he was also leaving EXO. He had missed recent concerts due to health issues, and rumours had spread, so

> It seemed Luhan could carry off any hair colour or style – swept-back pink, tumbling red curls or messy neon orange.

it was not a complete shock. He gave similar reasons to Kris for leaving and fans rallied to his support, with #alwayssupportluhan trending on Twitter worldwide.

To be fair, Luhan clearly made the right choice for himself, and hasn't looked back. Within months of leaving EXO he was filming a lead role in the Chinese comedy movie *20 Once Again*. When it was released in January 2015 it was a box-office smash in China and the theme tune, 'Our Tomorrow', which he recorded, was a number one hit (the video was watched a million times in just forty minutes). Over the next three years he would star in several other major movies, including the box-office triumph *Time Raiders* and *The Great Wall*, in which he co-starred with Matt Damon.

In 2015, Luhan also set up his own music studio. His first album, *Reloaded*, went double platinum, selling over 2 million copies. Then in October 2016 he began a series of mini-albums, dropped every two months through to his twenty-seventh birthday in April 2017. Each one sold over a million copies.

You can't miss Luhan in China. He appears on billboards and TV ads, his name associated with everything from KFC to the VW Beetle, and he even has a celebrity girlfriend in Guan Xiaotong, one of the most famous actresses in the country. In 2015, he entered the *Guinness Book of World Records* when a Weibo post he had made in 2012 (an innocuous comment on the Manchester United football team) accumulated more than 100 million comments. And, in 2017, *Forbes* business magazine named him the second-highest-earning male celebrity in China.

> In 2017, *Forbes* business magazine named Luhan the second-highest-earning male celebrity in China.

When he left EXO, Luhan continued to follow most his former bandmates on Instagram. He has hinted that he is still in touch with Xiumin, has sent birthday wishes to Tao, and when his warm reunion with Lay during the Bazaar Star Charity event in 2017 was filmed and shared online many EXO-Ls cried tears of joy. They might miss their 'Little Deer', but few begrudge him the success he has made of his career.

TAO

FACT FILE

Name: Huang Zitao

Stage name: Tao/Z.Tao

Date of birth: 2 May 1993

Birthplace: Qingdao, China

Nationality: Chinese

Height: 1.83 metres (6'0")

Position in EXO: rapper, vocalist

Sub-unit(s): EXO-M

Date left EXO: April 2015

EXO superpower: time control

In his home town of Qingdao in China, where he was steadily gaining a reputation as a rapper, Huang Zitao had attended an SM Entertainment global casting event. This resulted in him boarding a plane (for the first time in his life) to fly to Korea. It was 2010 and he was barely eighteen years old when he arrived in Seoul. He knew no one, spoke no Korean and had to room with the group's manager in order to learn the language quickly. Fortunately, Kris, also a Chinese-speaking trainee, had already been at SM for a couple of years and was able to help him settle in. As EXO took shape the two became close. Tao also became good friends with Sehun – they were two of the youngest members of the group – although the pair would soon be split up as Tao became the *maknae* in EXO-M and Sehun took the same role in EXO-K.

Back home, as well as rap, Zitao's passion had been for wushu, a Chinese martial art. He had won competitions in Qingdao and his dancing and fighting skills became a feature of EXO shows. Xiumin, who excelled in the Korean martial art taekwondo, and Tao would practise together in the dorm (Luhan said he got used to hearing Xiumin shout out in pain!).

It was as a martial-arts practitioner that Tao appeared in teaser number three, displaying acrobatic skills, spinning, kicking and wielding his wushu stick with some style. Fans would soon be calling him their 'Kung Fu Panda'. The third EXO member to be announced, his name was shortened to Tao and he was given the superpower ability of being able to control time. Much later in his career, Tao claimed that he did not feel ready to debut, that he had confessed as much to SM but had nevertheless carried on as part of the group.

Tao took his place in EXO-M as a rapper. Although he received

> Back home, as well as rap, Zitao's passion had been for wushu, a Chinese martial art. He had won competitions in Qingdao and his dancing and fighting skills became a feature of EXO shows.

fewer lines than Kris, many Exotics believed him the superior rapper and some even rated him above Chanyeol. Certainly, in EXO-M songs like 'Wolf', 'Two Moons', 'Growl' and 'Baby Don't Cry' he demonstrated a developing charisma and his singing added a great deal to the group's sound as well, as fans discovered in 'Peter Pan', 'Machine' and 'Baby'.

When Kris left the group, it was Tao who reacted with the greatest bitterness. In posts on Instagram and Weibo he wrote at length of how he felt betrayed by his former friend. However, a year later he expressed regret for his reaction, saying he had been shocked by Kris's sudden departure and he understood why Kris felt he needed to leave.

And then, on 23 April 2015, Tao's Weibo message – 'Sorry. Grateful.' – confirmed what many had already guessed. He, too, had left the group. His father's letter on the site implied he had persuaded his son to leave due to a lack of support over long-term injuries Tao had sustained during his martial-arts performances. Fans were upset, but not surprised, and his EXO bandmates still seemed to hold the EXO-M *maknae* in high esteem. Tao and Kris weren't publicly reconciled until December 2018 when they were spotted hugging at the Dragon TV New Year's Eve concert.

Like Kris and Luhan, Tao soon set out to build his career in China. By August he had released two successful solo mini-albums, *T.A.O* and *Z.TAO*, under the name Z.Tao. He had written the lyrics and music for the latter, and in 2016 it was as a singer-songwriter that he released his first studio album, *The Road*. The album included the track 'Hello, Hello', a collaboration with US rapper Wiz Khalifa, which was released as a single.

Tao also joined the other former members in pursuing an acting career. He co-starred with Jackie Chan in *Railroad Tigers* in 2016, and the following year appeared in the thriller *Edge of Innocence* and the martial-arts movie *The Game Changer*. He also played the lead role in the massively popular 2017 web drama *A Chinese Odyssey: Love You a Million Years*.

Tao may not yet have the achieved the mega-success of Kris and Luhan, but he is still a popular celebrity in China. He is an ambassador for Yves Saint Laurent and, on television, endeared himself to viewers with his open and honest appearance in a military reality show called *Takes a Real Man* and as the MC of the talent show *Produce 101*.

EXO-Ls were fascinated by one scene in *Produce 101* when he criticized contestants' attitudes and recalled his own trainee days.

> Tao is an ambassador for Yves Saint Laurent and, on television, endeared himself to viewers with his open and honest appearance in a military reality show called *Takes a Real Man*.

He said that, despite having no food to eat and living in an apartment with twenty other trainees, he never argued with or was jealous of the others, and it was clear he remembered his EXO days with pride and still valued what they had achieved together.

THIRTEEN

THE EXO WAVE

n South Korea it is called *hallyu*. In the West it is known as the Korean Wave. This refers to the global appeal of Korean culture, which has been steadily increasing since the end of the twentieth century. The term incorporates cosmetics, food and other products, but *hallyu* has been spearheaded by K-drama and K-pop, and turbo-charged by the growth of the internet and social media. For EXO and other K-pop acts, this has meant fans around the world are aware of their music, have watched the videos and have come to love them as much as the home-grown fans.

Outside Korea, SM had focused on building a fan base in China through EXO-M, but now three of the four Chinese members had left the group, leaving Lay as the sole Chinese representative. Would this affect EXO's popularity in China? The response to EXO Planet #2 – The EXO'luXion in the summer of 2015 suggested otherwise. The tour, with sets very similar to the Seoul shows in March, but incorporating the new tracks 'Love Me Right' and 'Promise', played eleven sold-out dates in six Chinese cities to a total audience of over 100,000 people.

Possibly worried that they might lose their last Chinese member, SM allowed Lay to set up his own studio in China and to promote himself as a solo artist and an actor, as well as remaining a member of EXO. He was on the way to becoming a massive star in his home country, and in September he released his autobiography, called *Standing Firm at 24*, which soon became a bestseller, and was cast in a leading role alongside Jackie Chan in a major movie, *Kung Fu Yoga*.

South Korea's Asian neighbours had always been at the forefront of *hallyu*, and had already taken EXO to their hearts. EXO's new tour took them to Taipei in Taiwan, Bangkok in Thailand and Hong Kong, and they played two nights in each city to audiences of more than 10,000. In each country and at each venue, the excitement was the same, with light sticks wielded, fan chants chanted, placards held aloft and screams accompanying every song.

What differentiated each performance was the way the members had fun with the fans. Some were surprised to hear Baekhyun speak Cantonese in Hong Kong and amused when he revealed that his knowledge of the language came from repeated viewings of the Hong Kong movie *Shaolin Soccer* – they were delighted when he sang the theme tune. And in Bangkok, Chanyeol took one of the hundreds of fan cards that read 'EXO-L will protect EXO', sat down on stage and changed the message to read 'EXO will protect EXO-L.'

In the midst of making new fans, EXO showed they hadn't forgotten their home support by returning to Seoul in September to play a solo show at the newly opened Gocheok Sky Dome. They would be the first artists to hold a concert in a Korean dome stadium and dedicated the show to the fans who had supported *Exodus* and *Love Me Right*, their second consecutive million-selling album. The event featured all the fan favourites, but especially memorable were the unique performances, which included Chanyeol singing John Legend's 'All of Me'; Chen, Xiumin and Baekhyun teaming up to cover SG Wannabe's 'As We Live'; and

> Some fans were surprised to hear Baekhyun speak Cantonese in Hong Kong and amused when he revealed that his knowledge of the language came from repeated viewings of the Hong Kong movie *Shaolin Soccer*.

D.O., accompanied by Chanyeol on guitar, delivering a beautiful version of Justin Bieber's 'Boyfriend'.

Since August, TV Tokyo, a popular channel in Japan, had been broadcasting weekly five-minute episodes of *EXO Channel*. The mixture of interviews, backstage footage and films of live performances proved a fabulous introduction to the group for Japanese fans. It also provided the perfect lead up to the EXO'luXion tour, which was due to hit the country for eight dates, including three each at the massive Tokyo and Osaka domes. As the filming schedule for *Kung Fu Yoga* clashed with the Japanese dates, SM permitted Lay to miss the concerts in Japan, although everyone was at great pains to point out that he was definitely still part of the group.

Cleverly, EXO picked this moment to drop their debut Japanese track, 'Love Me Right – Romantic Universe'. The single was a straightforward version of their Korean hit, but it was coupled on the CD with a Japanese original called 'Drop That', which found EXO rocking it up with a stomping party sound. With its 'Jump, jump, jump' chorus, it was a sure-fire live favourite from the very first play. 'Love Me Right' went straight to number one on the Japanese Oricon Chart and stayed there for two weeks. It broke the record for the highest first-week sales for any foreign artist's debut single. As far as K-pop was concerned, EXO were the kings of Japan.

Back home in South Korea, the big news was the forthcoming release of the new *Star Wars* movie, *The Force Awakens*. With EXO's extra-planetary back story and their use of *Star Wars*-style lightsabers in some of their stage performances, they were an obvious choice to help promote the movie. In fact, they did more than just promote, releasing a digital single and music video, 'Lightsaber', in collaboration with movie producers Disney. The song, recorded in Korean, Japanese and Chinese versions, didn't have quite the same impact on the charts as their other recent singles, but the solid EDM track with its catchy dubstep chorus and an impressive rap from Chanyeol was enough to enthuse the fandom.

The whole group contributed vocals, but the music video featured only Baekhyun, Kai and Sehun. Darth Vader's iconic heavy breathing starts the track, but aside from a 'Jedi-only' club and some fleeting lightsaber-wielding, the *Star Wars* setting is more of a background aesthetic than an overriding theme for the video, which seems to build to but never quite reach a dramatic climax. The boys looked good though: a blond Kai sporting a fresh cut on his cheek, a red-haired, baseball-jacketed Baekhyun angry in a convenience store and Sehun in a white leather jacket speeding along on a motorbike. Those enjoying the partnership were thrilled to find Suho, Chen, Kai and Sehun appearing alongside *Star Wars* memorabilia in a fun set of photos in the December 2015 issue of *Vogue Korea*.

In 2015, SM Entertainment involved many of their artists in work for UNICEF, the global children's charity. EXO, whose members had

> The boys looked good in the 'Lightsaber' music video: a blond Kai sporting a fresh cut on his cheek, a red-haired, baseball-jacketed Baekhyun angry in a convenience store and Sehun in a white leather jacket speeding along on a motorbike.

'Lightsaber' + 'Drop That' at MAMA 2015

After rocking the MAMA red carpet in their Prada knitwear (although the bunny print of Xiumin and Chanyeol's split opinion among fans), EXO stole the show at MAMA 2015 with their live performance. This was the night they proved they were worthy of the hype. They started with 'Lightsaber', which included some razor-edged choreography and a duel between Kai and Sehun, then went on to give a super-energetic display of 'Drop That', which they sang live, with D.O. and Chen in particular killing the vocals.

spent time volunteering in childcare centres even before their debut and had secretly funded various Korean and Chinese charities, were eager to assist with the partnership. They announced that part of the profits from the 2015 special winter release would go to Smile For U, an ongoing joint SM Entertainment and UNICEF project supporting music education for children in Asia.

After a fabulous set of teaser photos featuring black-and-white shots of each of the boys, thoughtful and smiling in plain turtleneck sweaters as snow gently fell, the mini-album was released on 10 December 2015. The comeback showcase took place in front of a few lucky fans at Lotte World, a theme park in Seoul, but people were also able to tune in via V Live, a video-streaming service that had been launched that summer.

In matching purple suits, the group sang 'Love Me Right' and three new songs from the Christmas EP, talked about making the video for the lead track, 'Sing for You', and showed a behind-the-scenes video of the photoshoot. They also took part in a quiz that led to loser D.O., along with Suho (who won and nominated himself to go along as well) having to ride the scream-inducing Viking ride at the theme park.

It was, however, Lay who shocked watching fans when he said, '2015 was not easy for EXO. The words I want to say to the members are sorry and I love you,' before being overwhelmed with tears and temporarily leaving the stage. Baekhyun explained, saying, 'Lay has been busy with his schedule in China, so he hasn't been able to be with us much. He doesn't have to be apologetic about it, but he always tells us that he's sorry. I think that's why he's crying.' The showcase set a new record for the V Live app, as 1.2 million people watched live and a similar number viewed the recording afterwards.

'Sing for You' is stripped-back EXO. It's a beautifully sung ballad with just a soft acoustic guitar accompaniment. It has few production effects and the simple arrangement relies on their voices (they all sing on the track), which really shine, especially Chen's vibrato and Chanyeol's soothing, low tones.

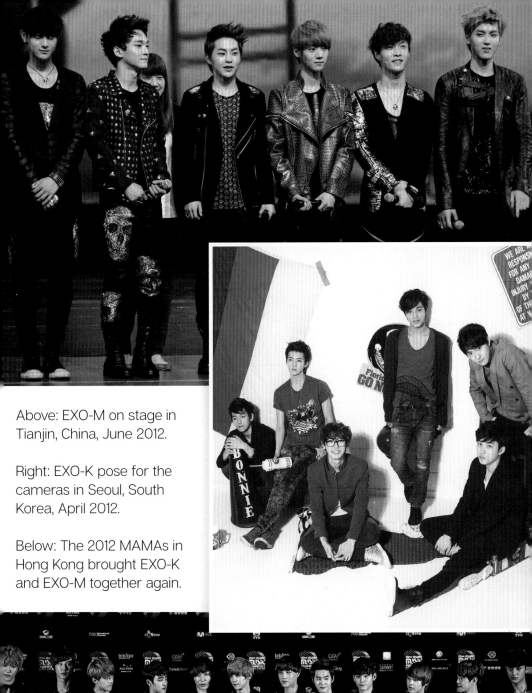

Above: EXO-M on stage in Tianjin, China, June 2012.

Right: EXO-K pose for the cameras in Seoul, South Korea, April 2012.

Below: The 2012 MAMAs in Hong Kong brought EXO-K and EXO-M together again.

SUHO

XIUMIN

LAY

BAEKHYUN

CHEN

CHANYEOL

D.O.

Their hair colours and styles may change, but they are always loved by millions around the world. Nine supremely talented individuals, together they form one of the world's greatest-ever boybands.

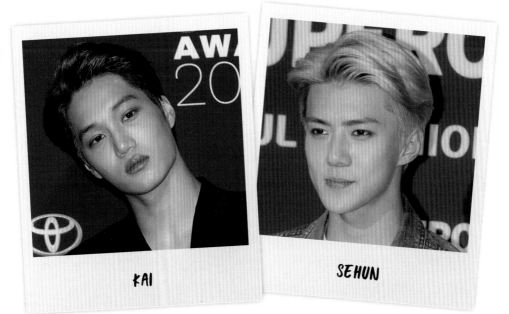

KAI

SEHUN

Above: Sporting those famous gold jackets at The EXO'luXion in Shanghai, China, May 2015.

Below: EXO on stage at the Gocheok Sky Dome in Seoul, South Korea, during their 'EXO – Love Concert in Dome' performance, October 2015.

Left: The 'Tree of Life' formation begins EXO's 'Wolf' choreography on MBC Music's *Show Champion*, Seoul, June 2013.

Above: Without Lay, the eight-member EXO took to the stage at the Gangnam Hanryu Festival in Seoul, South Korea, October 2015.

Below: EXO performing 'Monster' at the SBS K-Pop Super Concert in Suwon, South Korea, June 2016.

Above: EXO perform 'Monster' at MBC Korean Music Wave in Seoul, South Korea, October 2016.

Below: EXO strike a pose before their 'Dream Concert' in Seoul, South Korea, June 2017.

Above: 'We are one!' EXO promote their fourth album, *The War*, in Seoul, South Korea, July 2017.

Below: EXO steal the show at the Closing Ceremony of the 2018 Winter Olympics in Pyeongchang, South Korea, February 2018.

The music video, shot like the teasers in black and white, features the group together having fun and then, in contrast, alone in emotional turmoil and despair. It's powerful stuff, with Chanyeol and Suho engaging in a vicious fist fight; Kai mirroring their movements as he dances alone in the snow; D.O. screaming at the wheel of his car; and, somewhat bizarrely, Sehun as an astronaut floating in space, eventually being joined by a whale. Now, whales are often described as the loneliest of creatures, but some claimed this was a reference to the children's poem 'The Astronaut's Whale', about enduring friendship. Was the video alluding to the pain and eventual renewal caused by Kris, Luhan and Tao's departures? Many fans have come up with theories around this theme, but they remain just conjecture.

The whale and astronaut also featured on the artwork for the EP, which was released as usual in Korean and Chinese versions, each with five tracks. As well as the already released single, the EP included 'Lightsaber', the up-tempo 'Girl x Friend', the sensuous 'On the Snow' and a track the group would promote alongside 'Sing for You' called 'Unfair'. In the showcase, the boys had explained that both the latter songs would be lead tracks on the album because they couldn't choose between them. 'Unfair' is an upbeat, rolling pop song about a guy falling apart in front of a girl. Its place in EXO history was secured when it became the first K-pop song to make the iTunes 'Best of the Week' selection in the US.

'Unfair' became the first K-pop song to make the iTunes 'Best of the Week' selection in the US.

'Unfair' is thought of with great affection by EXO-Ls for two main reasons. One is the song's use of the word *eomaya*, which translates as 'oh my' and which became another fandom meme, especially after a later V Live broadcast where Sehun sang it over and over again in a very cute manner. Secondly, EXO promoted the song on *Music Core* where they gave a fantastic and much-loved performance in costume with D.O. as a baton-wielding police officer, Xiumin as a pilot, Suho as a taxi driver, Sehun a mechanic, Chanyeol a chef, Chen a fireman, Baekhyun a doctor and Kai as a racing driver, compete with crash helmet. While you're searching YouTube for that, you might also want to check out the *Inkigayo* performance, where they look super-cute in Santa outfits!

After a week, the Korean and Chinese versions sat at numbers one and two respectively in the Korean charts, breaking the then first-week sales record previously set by EXO's *Exodus* album by selling 267,900 copies. It reached number six in the Japanese Oricon Chart and number six in the US world charts, too. EXO would also notch up three more music-show trophies as they gained a triple crown on *Music Bank* over the festive period.

In the middle of the EP promotions and the ongoing EXO'luXion dates, which took them across South East Asia, came the awards season. They were still in Japan when the MMAs came around, although you wouldn't have guessed that they weren't present, as EXO-L fan chants rang around the Seoul Olympic Park Gymnastics Arena when they took the Album of the Year *daesang* for *Exodus*. And there was certainly no missing them at the MAMAs in early December, where they won Album of the Year for the third year in a row, picking up another *daesang*.

Lay was otherwise engaged again when the main new-year ceremonies came around, but EXO continued to collect the top trophies. The Seoul Music Awards, where they received the only grand prize, again for the third consecutive year, were marked by EXO-Ls encouraging the whole audience to sing 'Happy Birthday' to Kai and, to cap off the season, another hat-trick of *daesangs* was secured at the Golden Disc Awards. There, the speeches demonstrated the group's modesty, as Chen stated he thought EXO could still improve; their love of EXO-L, to whom they dedicated the win; and their care for each other – in this case, their concern for Xiumin, who had injured his leg in the annual *Idol Star Athletics Championships* football match.

EXO had begun 2016 sensationally; they had a hit album and had picked up *daesangs* at all the major ceremonies. Lay had been absent at times, but he remained committed to the group and all the others had acting, TV presenting, stage shows and other activities to keep them busy when their EXO schedules allowed. The New Year promised so much. They were about to take the EXO'luXion tour to North America for their first shows on the continent, and at the Golden Disc Awards Suho had promised a new album – well, he had assured fans there would be one sometime between January and December anyway! These truly were exciting times…

CHEN

FACT FILE

Name: Kim Jong-dae

Stage name: Chen

Date of birth: 21 September 1992

Birthplace: Siheung, South Korea

Nationality: South Korean

Height: 1.73 metres (5'8")

Position in EXO: vocalist

Sub-unit(s): EXO-M, EXO-CBX

EXO superpower: lightning

FOURTEEN

CHEN

The popular Korean Sunday-evening TV show *King of Mask Singer* has an interesting format in which well-known stars are heavily disguised in elaborate costumes, using imaginative stage names to keep their identity a secret while singing in the competition. The very first series, in 2015, featured a character called 'Legendary Guitarman' – a man singing Jeon Ram-hwi's 'Drunken Truth' with his face covered by a glittering gold guitar mask.

The Guitarman won through the first round, but was eliminated at the next and forced to disclose his identity. To the shock of the panel he was unmasked as EXO's Chen, the biggest star the series had seen. He said he had just been curious to see how people would react to his voice not knowing him as Chen from EXO. It proved, as if we didn't know already, that Chen's singing was heavenly – and also that this boy liked a joke.

> The Guitarman won through the first round of *King of Mask Singer*, but was eliminated at the next and forced to disclose his identity. To the shock of the panel he was unmasked as EXO's Chen, the biggest star the series had seen.

Kim Jong-dae grew up in Siheung, a city just 30km (20 miles) from Seoul. As he approached the end of his high-school years, he was already an accomplished singer – a claim backed up by a YouTube video of him singing with a young music-academy band. He was eighteen when his vocal instructor suggested he try out at an SM audition. He later admitted that the idea of being an idol singer hadn't initially appealed to him, but SM group SHINee's 'Please, Don't Go' had changed his mind, so he happily took up the suggestion.

It was at this audition that Jong-dae befriended and battled with Baekhyun for a place as a trainee with the company. In May 2011 he arrived at SM Entertainment and met up with Baekhyun again. Both had been selected and his new friend had arrived just a few days earlier. Like Baekhyun, he would have just a few months' training before being selected for EXO. However, Jong-dae was much nearer to the finished article than his soon-to-be bandmate.

On 29 December 2011, just six months after he had joined SM, Chen appeared in the SM Town stage on the end-of-year TV special *Gayo Daejeon*. Kai, Luhan and Tao also appeared, but it was Chen who was given a solo among the star-studded line-up. Totally confident, wearing a suit and a trilby, he blasted out thirty seconds of an operatic number – although it was only that morning that he had been formally introduced as the fourth member of EXO and he had yet to be seen in a teaser.

In February he appeared, all too briefly, in teaser number nineteen. By then he had already featured in EXO-M's first prologue single, 'What Is Love'. He sang beautifully, especially considering he was singing in Mandarin and had been learning the language for only a short time (although it was his pronunciation of the English word 'girl' as 'gull' that fans found funny!). Despite being South Korean, he had volunteered to be in the Chinese EXO and was given the popular Chinese name Chen as a stage name – possibly a nod to Edison Chen, a superstar rapper and actor.

Chen immediately became an integral member of EXO's fun trio, aka the beagle line, with Baekhyun and Chanyeol. Within the group he was known for his hyper behaviour and his fondness for playing pranks, but also for his considerate nature. In a *ViVi* magazine interview,

EXO members were asked which of the group they considered to be the most caring and every member chose Chen. He seems to be able to get along with anyone; he roomed with Lay in Korea and then Kris in China in order to improve his Mandarin, but also made good friends in other SM groups, including Super Junior's Ryeowook and Jonghyun and Onew from SHINee.

Fans grew to love the singer for his cute smile and the way his tongue poked out when he laughed. He had a reputation for being the chattiest at fan signings (he claimed he practised signing his name without looking so he could maintain eye contact with fans), and they noticed how he was always on hand to help upset or injured members when on stage. Early on, they gave him the nickname 'Dance Machine' after a fan shouted it at a signing – it was probably ironic but it stuck. Dancing wasn't Chen's forte, but, of course, he was working hard to improve it and he was a fast learner.

Anyway, it was his voice that was the main attraction. From debut, Chen was considered to have one of the best K-pop voices of his generation and it has continued to improve. His rich tenor tones are controlled and powerful, but he can also switch to a falsetto and hold the high notes (just listen to 'Drop That' or the 'Wolf' remix at EXO'rDIUM for proof). His contributions were sometimes overlooked before the groups merged, as most fans listened to EXO-K, but nonetheless quite a number expressed a preference for EXO-M versions; 'Black Pearl', 'Heart Attack', 'Thunder', 'Miracles in December' and 'My Lady' are often cited as songs where Chen's vocals really lift the track.

> From debut, Chen was considered to have one of the best K-pop voices of his generation and it has continued to improve. His rich tenor tones are controlled and powerful, but he can also switch to a falsetto and hold the high notes.

The departure of the three Chinese members, especially Luhan, changed the EXO dynamic and raised Chen's profile in the group. His Mandarin pronunciation was now rated the highest of all the South Korean members and, as OT9 came together, his live performances were stunning. While it was his high notes that often gained the attention of fans, it was his crystal-clear vocals, capable of delivering emotion and excitement, that were at the heart of so many EXO tracks.

With OT9, Chen's interest in songwriting started to come to the fore and he helped provide lyrics for 'Promise' on the *Love Me Right* repackage. The words to 2016's 'She's Dreaming' on *Lotto* were his alone, and he paints a totally imaginative and romantic picture of appearing as the moon in the dream of a girl he loves. On *The War*, he contributed lines to 'Ko Ko Bop' and 'Touch It', telling *Billboard*, 'I play out the lyrics in my mind as if it is like a scene from a movie.' However, he took his writing to another level on the poetic 'Lights Out' on the 2017 *Universe* EP and, with Chanyeol, on 2018's 'Love Shot'. Both tracks are deep explorations of the meaning of love.

In September 2015, those who had loved watching a masked Chen sing solo on *King of Mask Singer* were soon able to see him on stage again. Alongside other K-pop stars such as Infinite's Dongwoo and Sunggyu, SHINee's Key and f(x)'s Luna, Chen was cast as Benny in the Seoul production of the Lin-Manuel Miranda musical *In the Heights*. His performance was well-received and he enjoyed the experience, but that has been his only acting appearance to date.

During a press conference for the 2013–14 variety show *EXO Showtime*, Chen had teased fans by promising to sing if the show's viewer ratings exceeded 1.2 per cent (viewing figures in South Korea are always expressed as a percentage). When ratings went well above this, he kept his promise and in the seventh episode sang a beautiful cover of the ballad 'Nothing Better'. Fans who saw it were soon demanding a Chen solo and, in August 2015, their wish was granted.

His first solo release, 'Best Luck', was an OST for a TV drama called

It's Okay, That's Love, which he was happy to support as it starred D.O. as a high-school student and aspiring author. Chen sings with perfect tenderness and it was reported that he delivered the song in one take – quite a feat for such a difficult solo. It not only broke the top ten in Korea, but also melted the hearts of both fans and new listeners.

Over the next few years Chen earned himself another nickname: the 'OST King'. A duet called 'Everytime' with the female singer Punch (who would also work with Chanyeol) for the TV series *Descendants of the Sun* went to number one in Korea; 'Beautiful Accident', a powerful ballad for a Chinese movie of the same name, was a hit for him and Suho; and he teamed up with Baekhyun and Xiumin in 'For You', a pre-CBX hit and OST for the 2016 TV series *Moon Lovers: Scarlet Heart Ryeo*.

> Over the next few years Chen earned himself another nickname: the 'OST King'.

In an interview with Korean magazine *Singles*, Chen described his approach to OSTs. He explained how he tries to understand the message of the song rather than the drama itself, approaching it as a musician rather than an actor, and saying, 'I believe that if I fully understand the lyrics and sing with an honest mind then the song will fit the scene well.' Such a method has certainly worked in his recent solo OSTs. A tear-jerking ballad called 'I'm Not Okay' for the drama *Missing 9* in 2017 and 'Cherry Blossom Love Song' from *100 Days My Prince* (also starring D.O.) both enhanced his reputation as the OST King.

SM Entertainment also gave Chen opportunities to show off his vocal skills outside EXO. He had three tracks on the second album of their 2014 SM the Ballad project, including the Chinese version of the title track, 'Breath', with Chinese singer Zhang Liyin, and 'A Day Without You' with SHINee singer Jonghyun. Both tracks made the Gaon top ten in South Korea.

Chen also featured in collaborations in the digital-release project SM Station. The pick of these are a 2016 venture into EDM with DJ Alesso

Immortal Song 2 – Chen and Baekhyun – 'Really I Didn't Know'

In the Korean Saturday-evening show *Immortal Songs: Singing the Legend*, K-pop artists compete against each other by singing different songs from the repertoire of legendary artists. The episode broadcast on 17 August 2013 saw six acts perform songs made famous by Jang Mi-hwa and Im Hee-sok. With their performance of 'Really I Didn't Know', Chen and Baekhyun alerted a nation just waking up to 'Growl' that these good-looking boys had beautiful voices too. As for Chen, he proved that he could go high or low with incredible intensity. It's an awesomely powerful performance – and the boys really should have won!

called 'Years' (which was performed in EXO's ElyXiOn [dot] concerts) and 'Nosedive', a collaboration with Dynamic Duo. The latter contrasted Chen's sweet vocals with Duo's forthright rap in a motivational song about the importance of letting your emotions show in times of hardship. 'Nosedive' reached number two in the charts and the music video has amassed over 6 million views on YouTube.

In 2016, SM also launched the sub-unit EXO-CBX, with Chen the C alongside Baekhyun's B and Xiumin's X. The guys said the idea came about when their trainer in the gym remarked that they'd look good as a group as their heights were similar, prompting them to take the proposal for a sub-unit to SM. With CBX, Chen had fun with his friends with the upbeat 'Hey Mama!' and gave a luscious solo in 'Thursday' on *Blooming Days*; and, given the freedom to try something new, he hit fans with a rock track in 'Watch Out' on the Japanese album.

Chen even felt free enough to experiment with an auburn mullet in EXO-CBX's 'Blooming Days' music video. Remember, this is the guy who had previously been the one EXO member to stay away from the bottles of bright hair dye, preferring to stick to shades of brown and short periods of black. *The War* comeback in 2017 unleashed the blond Chen (probably his most popular look ever) and then, for the 'Power' repackage, there he was in bright orange. It wasn't to everybody's taste, but it sure made fans sit up and take notice!

Anyway, Chen's beauty is more than skin deep. In fact, he might just be the nicest man in K-pop. In November 2018, the Idol Champ voting app ran a survey to discover which idol was the biggest 'Warm City Man' – a Korean term for someone who has a big heart and smile. Chen pulled in 45 per cent of the votes – easily the most of all the nominees. Indeed, the singer is known for his generosity to charities and volunteer organisations, sometimes secretly making donations of thousands of dollars.

> Chen's beauty is more than skin deep. In fact, he might just be the nicest man in K-pop.

Chen is often cited as the most overlooked member of EXO. Perhaps there's some truth in this due to the time he spent in EXO-M or maybe it took his emergence as OST King for his talents to be truly appreciated, but there can now be no doubt that his beautiful voice makes him an indispensable member of the vocal line, and his fun and kind nature enhance the charisma of both EXO and EXO-CBX. Chen is indeed a gem at the very heart of the group.

FIFTEEN

EXO GO USA

By 2016, K-pop had established a foothold in the US. Boosted by the million-plus Korean-Americans in the country, it had also been adopted by music fans from a whole range of other communities who took a liking to the freshness and vibrancy of the sound coming from across the Pacific. For more than a decade, the K-pop presence had grown, with artists such as Rain, Wonder Girls and Girls' Generation making an early impact before Psy's 'Gangnam Style' went viral in the summer of 2012.

Although some didn't consider Psy to be true K-pop, he did open a lot of people's ears (and minds) to Korean music. KCON, the *hallyu* convention founded in 2012, had its first outing in California in 2016 and top K-pop groups began to see opportunities not just in the US but across the continents, from Canada to Mexico and Brazil. 'Psy, Super Junior, Girls' Generation, TVXQ and SHINee *sunbaes* [elders] paved the way for us,' Suho said. 'It's our duty as *hoobae* [junior] groups to solidify K-pop's position in the world.'

Back in December, EXO had announced they were taking the EXO'luXion tour to North America. It wasn't their first trip across the Pacific – EXO-M had attended KCON in LA in 2012 and the whole group had made a real splash at the event a year later – but these five dates would be their first solo concerts on the continent. It wasn't a big gamble, though, because they knew there were plenty of EXO-Ls waiting to see them. They had topped the *Billboard* World Albums chart, held the record for the biggest-ever sales week for a K-pop album in the US, and 'Call Me Baby' had even broken into the Canada Hot 100.

The tour took in five stops in North America, with locations decided via a poll carried out by concert-crowdsourcer site MyMusicTaste. Despite some controversy over how it was conducted, the chosen cities were New York, Chicago, Dallas, Los Angeles and Vancouver. Once again, however, Lay was absent, as he was busy with solo activities in China, and they even started the tour with just seven members when Kai was delayed because of visa issues.

EXO played to over 40,000 people across the five cities, selling out in LA, Chicago and New York (although the concert hall was actually in Newark, New Jersey, half an hour away from central New York), and playing to almost full houses in Dallas and Vancouver. The EXO'luXion set list was updated to include 'Drop That', and they brought in 'Sing For You' and 'Unfair' for the encore. Suho took the lead in speaking English and the audiences, many of whom had followed the group for years, were wild and excited. Indeed, for some it became known as the 'One Step Back' tour after a chant instigated by the group at some venues to prevent the crush that developed at the front of the auditorium.

> EXO played to over 40,000 people across the five cities, selling out in LA, Chicago and New York.

It was clear that the members enjoyed their eleven days in America. Most of them shared pictures and video clips on social-media sites, and seemed to revel in being able to wander around and even ride on public transport without being recognized. Chanyeol said later, 'Being able to go out with Suho and Sehun, I really felt the American culture... It was really fun.'

It was a whirlwind tour, but the enthusiastic reaction of US and Canadian fans confirmed that K-pop was thriving in North America. US K-pop expert Jeff Benjamin wrote on the Fuse.tv website that 'Even without forcefully pushing their individual identities, promoting much in America or even learning the language… EXO is proving that Asian music is heating up in the US.'

As the tour was finally coming to a close, EXO returned to Asia for concerts in Jakarta in Indonesia, Dalian in China, and Kuala Lumpur in Malaysia, before the final three-night EXO'luXion [dot] encore shows back home at the Olympic Gymnasium Arena in Seoul in mid-March. After forty-four concerts in a total of twenty-five regions around the world, they returned to where they had started almost exactly a year before. Lay was back and all nine were on stage, although poor Kai was on crutches after a dance injury and spent the performance sitting down.

Unsurprisingly, there was a party atmosphere at these encore shows. This was especially true on the last date, when they appeared on stage in cute animal onesies to play a random dance game, with Lay determined to do an adult-rated dance and the rest of them piling on top to stop him. They closed the show with 'Promise' and it was left to Suho to wrap up, saying, 'This is the end of EXO'luXion [dot], but the history of EXO will go on. The history won't be built by us alone, but something we and our fans build together.'

However, it still wasn't quite finished! A few days later came the EXO'luXion [Epilogue], a screening and talk featuring SM's performance director Shim Jae-won and visual director Kwon Soon-wook. They told the story of how the tour had been produced, revealing fascinating details about how intricately the whole thing had been planned and explaining how the set had deliberately reflected the members' 'superpowers'; how when it had been suggested the boys changed on stage, Baekhyun had said, 'Hey! Are you trying to ruin us?'; and how EXO-Ls and their light sticks were incorporated into the set. Pure genius.

As April began, Kai, last seen on crutches and in tears at the emotional end of EXO'luXion, was back as the focus of EXO-L's attention. *Man Woo Jeol* (which translates as 'very foolish holiday') is the Korean equivalent of April Fools' Day and, as in the rest of the world, it's a day for pranks and fibs. For that reason, many took an SM announcement that Kai was dating Krystal from EXO's sister SM group f(x) as a joke. Gradually, though, they realized it was indeed true. The couple had been friends since they were trainees eight years before, but had only recently become aware of their feelings for each other.

They were said to have been skiing together and liked to visit top-class restaurants.

> Kai and Krystal had been friends since they were trainees eight years before, but had only recently become aware of their feelings for each other.

As people knew they were friends, rumours hadn't spread when they were spotted out together. The news, however, was not greeted with the same hostility that had surrounded Baekhyun and Taeyeon. Were EXO-Ls becoming more easy-going? Or did the fact that Kai had deleted his Instagram account in 2015 and rarely engaged with social media help him to avoid many of the bitter comments? Whatever the reason, the couple were able to continue their romance – whenever schedules allowed!

EXO'luXion [dot] Dance Relay in Animal Pajamas

You wouldn't think a group of men appearing on stage in onesies could cause such a stir! When the guys took the stage in animal costumes at the final EXO'luXion concert in Seoul in March 2016, EXO-Ls went crazy. Relaxed and playful, the members were funny, cute and sexy and their joking and teasing showed just how well they all got along. Just for the record: Suho is a rabbit; Sehun is a wolf; Kai is a bear (with a bad foot); Baekhyun is a flying squirrel; Chanyeol, a white tiger; Lay, of course, is a sheep; Xiumin, a cat; Chen, a dinosaur and D.O, a penguin. Awwww!

When they were not busy rehearsing and recording for the next comeback, every member of EXO had activities outside the group. These boys were talented and in demand. Back in January, Baekhyun had recorded a duet called 'Dream' with Suzy from Miss A. Almost old-school jazz and released with a classy music video, it topped the Korean charts for weeks and won a triple crown on *Inkigayo*. D.O. starred in his first movie, *Pure Love* (also released as *Unforgettable*), and Suho also made his film debut in *Glory Day* (aka *One Way Trip*). Chanyeol starred in and sang the theme to the romantic-comedy movie *So I Married an Anti-fan*, while Kai appeared in *Choco Bank*, one of the most popular South Korean web dramas ever broadcast.

Chen also had a number one duet, 'Everytime', the soundtrack for the TV drama *Descendants of the Sun*, with singer Punch; Baekhyun began his acting career with *Seondal: The Man Who Sells the River*; Xiumin released a single, 'Call You Bae', with rapper Jimin from girl group AOA; and Sehun was cast in his first movie, *Catman*. This was all in addition to fan meetings, group-anniversary and birthday celebrations, brand ambassadorships (EXO were associated with Lotte Duty Free, Nature Republic, Skechers footwear and other products) and TV appearances.

Over in China, Lay was really making a name for himself as an actor, songwriter and solo singer. He was a regular cast member of the

Love Me Right – *Fantastic Duo*

This is something different and fun. In May 2016, six of the group came together on a TV show called *Fantastic Duo* where fans compete to duet with their favourite act. A singer called Jeolla Province Red Pants (yep, for real) won the chance to sing with EXO. Although she does well, it is the boys we are watching. Singing with a live band, they are relaxed, smiling and having a great time, without stealing the spotlight.

Chinese variety show *Go Fighting!*, had made his formal big-screen debut in *Oh My God* and starred in the TV series *To Be a Better Man*, while 'Monodrama', which he co-wrote, topped the Chinese charts for five weeks.

EXO had also been busy preparing for their comeback. Their third full album, *Ex'Act*, was released on 9 June with double title tracks, 'Monster' and 'Lucky One'. The teaser photoshoots had prepared fans for the double take. The 'Lucky One' pictures – with a lucky four-leaf-clover-style EXO logo – were almost overexposed and showed the group in colourful but faded, classic comfy clothes. Each of the boys has a distracted, just-woken-up look. Chanyeol's flaming red locks, Kai's blond curls, Baekhyun's freckles and Xiumin's dirty-pink hair were notable, with D.O. and Sehun rocking the bespectacled look.

The 'Monster' images, on the other hand, were a complete contrast. Altogether darker and more sinister, as symbolized by an EXO logo made from bones, the members wore black and were photographed in shadow, looking intense and troubled. Chanyeol's lip tattoo, Sehun and Lay's voluptuous lips and Baekhyun's wet-look black hair set the tone in these sensuous images full of saturated black eye makeup, chains and piercings.

The album, along with the music videos for the two lead tracks, dropped on 9 June 2016. Incredibly, 666,000 copies had been pre-ordered by the time it was released. They were pretty sure it would top the charts, and even promised to upload a video of five-year-old Xiumin dancing if they won a music show.

> *Ex'Act*, along with the music videos for the two lead tracks, dropped on 9 June 2016. Incredibly, 666,000 copies had been pre-ordered by the time it was released.

The stomping and funky 'Lucky One' is a smoothly produced piece of catchy electro-pop, with the raps, harmonies and choruses effortlessly blending into each other. The song, with lines given to all the members, utilizes a synth-flute sound and strong beat as it tells how it's worth climbing every obstacle to find the one you love.

The music video finds the members being kept against their will in another maze, this time in a hospital. The dystopian sterile effect is emphasized by the boys' shiny, pale faces and all-white outfits. Only when they are being experimented on do they regain their superpowers (when discussing the video on the *Music Bank* TV show, Baekhyun joked that they had lost them because it had been so long since they had used them!) and manage to escape. But for all its sci-fi, futuristic spy style, the video is not without humour, especially Kai preferring to dance rather than use his transportation power – which, naturally, makes the nurse's head explode.

'Monster', a song about an all-consuming and all-controlling love, takes us back to the vibe of 'Mama' and 'Overdose' with an EDM and hip-hop mix that is given the darkest of treatments. There is such drama and power in the vocals. Baekhyun and Chen provide the clout, which carries the song over the electronic wails and insistent beat through to Chanyeol and Sehun's impressive rap break and Baekhyun's sign-off. It's a classic EXO track, which sweeps you off your feet, spirits you through swells and surges, and finally sets you gently down again.

The 'Monster' music video follows aesthetically from the teaser photos: dressed in black with accompanying chains, piercings, cuts and bruises, they are rebels fighting a repressive police force. They are coming off worse until double agent Baekhyun helps them escape. These stylish and exciting scenes are intercut with some of the group's most impressive choreography yet, devised by the acclaimed

> If they were anxious, the reaction of fans around the world would reassure them pretty quickly. After just twenty-four hours, the music video for the Korean version of 'Monster' had racked up a record-breaking 4.5 million views on YouTube.

NappyTabs, who had previously worked with Madonna, Christina Aguilera and BoA.

At the showcase for the album, Suho admitted that there had been some concern about how the track and video would be received. 'I wouldn't say we weren't sure, but we were slightly worried about "Monster", he said. If they were anxious, the reaction of fans around the world would reassure them pretty quickly. After just twenty-four hours, the music video for the Korean version of 'Monster' had racked up a record-breaking 4.5 million views on YouTube, with the Chinese version amassing a further 1.5 million. There was no doubt the boys had produced yet another massive hit.

CHANYEOL

FACT FILE

Name: Park Chan-yeol

Stage name: Chanyeol

Date of birth: 27 November 1992

Birthplace: Seoul, South Korea

Nationality: South Korean

Height: 1.86 metres (6'1")

Position in EXO: rapper, vocalist

Sub-Unit(s): EXO-K

EXO superpower: fire

SIXTEEN

CHANYEOL

For those new to EXO, Chanyeol is easy to pick out in the blurred whirl of dancers. Since Kris left the group he is the tallest of all the members. Indeed, everything about the group's rapper is writ large: he has big eyes and a huge smile that reveals very straight, white teeth, earning him the nickname 'The Nation's Good Teeth' or, fans' favourite, 'Rich Teeth' or 'Wealthy Teeth'. He also has quite large ears (but keep that quiet – supposedly D.O. once made fun of Chanyeol's ears and Chanyeol wouldn't talk to him for a month!). When asked about his features by the Japanese magazine *Nonno*, Chanyeol said, '[I like] everything. I think my eyes and ears really set me apart, though.'

Chanyeol has a pretty huge personality, too. He's the one falling off his chair in hysterics, pulling the most shocked face possible or acting like the most surprised guy ever. Such behaviour in an early TV appearance on variety show *Happy Camp* led to him being dubbed the group's 'Reaction King'. It was and still is a nickname that fans like to use, although the simple 'Yeollie' is cuter, but he is most often known as the self-appointed 'Happy Virus' of EXO. He insists he never gets

> Chanyeol has a pretty huge personality, too. He's the one falling off his chair in hysterics or pulling the most shocked face possible, which led to him being dubbed the group's 'Reaction King'.

angry, no matter how difficult the situation. Famously he once said, 'I will always be positive and smile like an idiot' – and for that alone he is loved by millions.

Chanyeol and his sister Park Yoo-ra, three years his senior, grew up in South Korea's capital, Seoul. Park Yoo-ra is now a news anchor for Korean twenty-four-hour news channel YTN and has remained supportive of her idol brother's career – she introduces news reports about EXO's success with glee! Chanyeol has also remained close to his parents. He has even helped his mother open a pasta restaurant called Viva Polo (which is decorated with EXO memorabilia) and enabled his father to start a burger café whose name translates as 'Make a Good World'. There you can buy both a Chan burger and a Yeol burger!

Naturally a happy child, Chanyeol's career began with a love of music in elementary school. Watching the movie *School of Rock* at a young age inspired him to learn to play the drums, and by middle school he was playing with friends in a rock band called Heavy Noise. Rock was his music genre of choice, with Green Day, Nirvana and X-Japan among his favourite groups. However, when he appeared with the school band he really got the singing bug as he enjoyed performing with others and relished the buzz of the audience's applause.

By high school, the young, round-faced boy had grown into a tall, handsome youth. His parents had enrolled him in acting school and in 2008 he took part in the televised *Smart Model Contest* where he showed off his guitar playing, beatboxing and modelling skills, and took second place. Then, on the way home from school one day, he was spotted by a SM streetcaster and invited to audition.

In a 2018 video call on Mnet's *New Music*, fellow artist Tak Jae-hoon asked Chanyeol if it was difficult to get into SM Entertainment. Always ready with a cheeky quip, EXO's rapper replied, 'No. You just ask security to open the door!' When he started as an SM trainee in 2008, though, Chanyeol was still at school and was rather surprised by the stir it caused among his classmates. He has admitted that this did cause him to become a little subdued for the first time in his life – but not for long!

He would spend four years as a trainee before debuting, yet Chanyeol has never expressed any regrets or complaints. His deep love of music and a desire to learn seem to have seen him through the hard graft. His musical tastes also broadened. He expressed a liking for singer-songwriter Jason Mraz and rap superstar Eminem and, through fellow SM group TVXQ, he gained an understanding and appreciation of K-pop idol music.

He might have begun his traineeship hoping to be a rock star, but that was never going to happen at SM. His good looks and all-round musical talent earmarked him as an idol star and he appeared in two Girls' Generation music videos. He had a part topping and tailing 'Genie' and a shorter cameo as the main paparazzi in 'Twinkle' (from GG sub-unit TTS), but these were enough to get him noticed by keen-eyed viewers.

He also focussed on becoming a rapper, a role he relished and was prepared to work at. However, there was one area in which he did struggle: dance. He worked hard at it, but even approaching debut feared he would be seen as the 'black hole' in the 'Mama' choreography. He thanked Kai and Sehun for helping him reach the standard required for debut and since then his dance skills have continued to improve.

Chanyeol was always one of the more extrovert characters in the dorm, but he really came to life when his beagle-line partners-in-crime, Chen and Baekhyun, joined SM in 2010. Kai remarked how when Baekhyun joined, the dorm suddenly became noisy as Chanyeol hit it off with the newcomer immediately. And if Baekhyun became the friend he would mess around with, his other close friend, D.O., soon became the one with whom Chanyeol could share his worries, particularly as they took the same subway when they went home and found plenty of time to talk.

Chanyeol became the twelfth and final member of EXO to be formally introduced by SM. On 23 February 2012 he appeared in

Chanyeol became the twelfth and final member of EXO to be formally introduced by SM.

teaser number twenty. Dressed in a long raincoat, with his side-parted hair falling over his right eye, he investigated an old barn. He seemed intense, quiet and thoughtful, the silent type. How wrong can you be! His teaser would become one of the most viewed of all, mainly because of the backing song 'El Dorado', which fans took to their hearts just as much as they did the figure in the raincoat with the amazing smile.

It didn't take long to get to know the real Chanyeol. In interviews and variety shows, in a group of shy, nervous boys, his confidence and exuberance stood out. And he was receiving attention from fans, too. Often it was his cute baby face that got him noticed, but he also became the source of some rather, well, cringe-worthy memes. This was especially true of the performance of 'Two Moons' at EXO's debut showcase where his opening line of 'Ayyo waddup Kreese!' became a fandom in-joke and, of course, in 'Growl' Chanyeol was responsible for the immortal cry of '*Chogiwa*!'

He also became the self-proclaimed 'Three Minutes and One Second Guy'. In the 'Growl' music video, there is no sign of Chanyeol until a second over three minutes in. On the *Happy Together* show he explained that when he finally did appear on the video, many sat up and thought, 'Who is this handsome guy?' The host then asked him how many times he had watched the video – to which he gave a typically honest Chanyeol reply: 'Probably four to five hundred times, but only that one part, because I only appear there!'

With such charisma and confidence, Chanyeol was a natural MC and variety-show cast member. He was appointed MC of EXO's reality show *EXO's Showtime* and was soon co-hosting TV music and awards programmes. In 2018 Chanyeol MC'd the 2018 *Gayo Daechukje* show alongside Dahyun from TWICE and Jin from BTS – with fans especially enjoying seeing him get on so well with a boy from a so-called rival group. Reality shows such as *Law of the Jungle, Roommate* and *Master Key* also helped fans discover more about the idol and, in 2018, along with Girls' Generation's Sunny, he explored California in the food travel show *Salty Tour*. Whatever the show, Chanyeol has always been good company.

However, that is not to undervalue his contribution to EXO's music and performances. As a rapper he has been integral to the groups' songs. His technique has improved over the years, but he has always shown an amazing versatility and has used his rasping voice to full effect. From 'Full Moon' and 'Lightsaber' to 'Lucky', 'Tempo' and, of course, 'Promise', he has shown he can deliver tender, sexy, fast and emotional raps. His deep baritone singing voice has also enhanced many EXO tracks, with 'Don't Go', 'White Noise', 'Exodus' and '24/7' among the shining examples. In live performances, Chanyeol provides the extra; his guitar playing, drumming, DJing and, naturally, his interactions with fans make an EXO show without him unthinkable.

> As a rapper, Chanyeol has been integral to the groups' songs. His technique has improved over the years, but he has always shown an amazing versatility and has used his rasping voice to full effect.

Ever since 2015's 'Run', Chanyeol has been contributing lyrics for EXO tracks. These include great songs such as 'Heaven', 'Ko Ko Bop' and 'Love Shot'. He has great poetic skills and writes with fun and humour, but he is also able to display an honest and sensitive side. 'Sweet Lies', which tells of his fear of being hurt in a relationship, is one such song; 'With You', which draws on his relationship with fans, is another; while the live song 'Hand' remains an extraordinarily frank tribute to his fellow members.

Outside EXO, Chanyeol has had a series of successful collaborations and has featured on various vocalists' tracks. Highlights among these are his fabulous rap verse for a song called 'Rewind' by Zhou Mi of Super Junior-M (the band's Chinese sub-unit) in 2014; 'Freal Luv', a 2016 collaboration with the Far East Movement, Tinashe and DJ Marshmello, which Chanyeol also helped write and compose; and the inspiring upbeat anthem 'We Young' in which he duets with Sehun (it also has a gorgeous music video featuring both of them).

'Multi-talented' is the phrase often associated with Chanyeol. On top of the rapping and songwriting, he can play guitar, drum, bass and djembe (a West African style of drum), and is a good sportsman – he won the bowling gold medal at the 2018 *Idol Star Athletics Championships*. He also has a creative mind. He is reportedly responsible for coming up with EXO's original hexagon logo and is taking an interior design graduate course at Inha University. He can add acting to the list of his accomplishments too, having starred in the 2016 movie *So I Married an Anti-fan* and appearing in *EXO Next Door* plus the TV dramas *Missing 9* and *Memories of the Alhambra*.

He doesn't actually need to do much for fans to adore him. He manages to look good in virtually every comeback and can effortlessly rock red, black and silver hair. Fans especially loved the pink backcomb of 'Ko Ko Bop' and the shaggy grey-brown of 'Call Me Baby'. It was no surprise, then, that he was able to rekindle his teenage modelling career; and when he attended Tommy Hilfiger's autumn 2017 show in London, *Vogue* magazine wrote that he stole the spotlight the moment he arrived – adding that no one wore the Tommy look better than Chanyeol.

Chanyeol and Punch – 'Stay With Me'

According to *Billboard* and YouTube, this video was the third-most-watched music video in the world in December 2016. It was originally an OST for the incredibly popular K-drama *Goblin*, but stands alone as a beautiful track – as its 130 million views attest. Here Chanyeol not only shows his rap skills, but also puts his vocals on display, matching the sweet and beautiful tones of his female co-singer, Punch. This is serious Chanyeol, putting out the emotion without the smiles and waves – until the very end, that is.

Putting his dreamy looks to one side for a moment, fans have found so much about their Yeollie to love. He is the group's Instagram king, regularly providing them with fun photographs and updates, and in December 2018 he quickly became the most-followed Korean celebrity on Instagram, with over 16 million followers. He is a dog lover who even opened an Instagram account for his adorable puppy Toben (it amassed 72,000 followers in its first ten hours!). And he is so kind to his fellow members. In 2017, he bought them all gaming laptops because he thought it was good for teamwork if they played the game *PlayerUnknown's Battlegrounds* together!

> In 2017 Chanyeol bought all the EXO members gaming laptops because he thought it was good for teamwork if they played the game *PlayerUnknown's Battlegrounds* together!

For their part, Chanyeol's fans are among the most passionate and have raised money for a $2,000 Rolex to be presented to him and a garden-style forest within the World Cup Park in Seoul to be created in his name. In 2017, the Chanyeol fansite *Yeolmaefarm* even fundraised for legal fees and took out a lawsuit against malicious online commenters (with Chanyeol's approval) after they had spent years collecting evidence. That's the kind of super-loyal fandom you get when you're super-fun, super-handsome and totally super-talented.

And every year those dedicated fans also look forward to Chanyeol's Halloween fancy dress. He has been a fabulously sexy Joker and won the 2017 SM Town Halloween competition with an amazing Iron Man costume (which he confessed cost him the entire contents of his bank account!). However, he didn't return in 2018 to defend his title because his costume didn't make it through customs in time. He was, apparently, devastated, but took the opportunity to show off his new costume a month later, on his birthday, when he hosted a special event for fans. When he appeared in a superb Deadpool suit everyone agreed that he would definitely have won again had the outfit arrived in time for Halloween.

Chanyeol is also one of a select number of K-pop idols to have a tattoo. In fact, he has more than one. He has a monkey tattoo, two guitars in the shape of crescents and 'LOEY' ('yeol' backwards) on a finger, but the one that drove fans wild was a small, stamp-style tattoo on his wrist that reads 'L-1485'. In November 2018, he explained that the 'L' stood for EXO-L and the number refers to 5 August 2014, the date on which EXO's fan club was first created. He then touched every fan's heart by adding, 'All of you will always be a part of my body until the day I die.'

SEVENTEEN

DANCING KINGS

EXO's international fan base had been growing hungry for more access to the members. They couldn't watch Korean TV, so their opportunities to see EXO were often restricted to music videos and random YouTube uploads. However, in June 2016, at the same time as the *Ex'Act* release, EXO delivered their own series on the V Live app and the Chinese streaming site YinYueTai. *Exomentary* comprised their comeback stage, fifteen personal broadcasts and, as a finale, a ten-pin bowling competition.

The individual shows lasted anything from forty-five minutes to well over an hour and were broadcast live, so the group's individual characters could come across more fully than ever before. Members chose their own themes and first up was Sehun's 'Please Take Care of My Puppy', starring the *maknae*'s own gorgeous Bichon Frise puppy called Vivi. The show was unintentionally hilarious, as Vivi refused to do anything he was told, and it got the series off to a flying start.

> 'Please Take Care of My Puppy', starring Sehun's own gorgeous Bichon Frise puppy called Vivi, was unintentionally hilarious, as Vivi refused to do anything he was told.

There were plenty more gems to follow. Suho revealed his 'skills' as a pastry chef; Chanyeol let us into his studio, showed off his amazing manga-character model collection and played his songs, including one he wrote using comments made by EXO-Ls, which was later posted on Instagram; D.O. taught us some home cooking, accompanied by sweet references to his mother; and Xiumin and Chen, billed as the Fantastic Kim Brothers, took to the karaoke mics, with Xiumin singing the song that had got him through the SM auditions. Other episodes had their own charm. 'Brunch with Lay' was less eating and more hearing his new compositions while Kai's slightly ponderous Q&A session was made bearable by him looking so good with blond hair and by Suho springing out, having hidden in the closet for twenty minutes!

While this was being devoured by EXO-Ls, the group were also busy promoting *Ex'Act* and its twin singles. The album was, as ever, released in Korean and Chinese versions, and the artwork featured a new logo, which used letters to form a hexagon with an X in the centre. Both versions came with photobooks containing either the dark 'Monster' images or the bright 'Lucky One' photos.

The album was another step forward for EXO. They were recording as one unit, and the tracks revealed a more mature sound. In the nine songs, including the two singles (which also featured as instrumental bonus tracks on the album), there were fewer attempts to experiment or to slip back into the comfort of production-heavy songs. Instead they developed an electronic house groove in songs such as 'Artificial Love', which features some great Sehun-Chanyeol interplay, and 'White Noise', where Chen's chorus shines. The more mature R&B sound brought a smooth touch to 'One and Only' and 'Cloud 9', and they finished on a powerful ballad, 'Stronger', which is not only beautifully sung but also astounding for the clarity of D.O.'s English pronunciation.

Two songs on the album are noteworthy beyond the musical content. 'Heaven', a more conventional rap-and-vocals combination, has emotive and moving lyrics written by Chanyeol – the first major contribution by one of the group to one of their own songs. Another number, 'They Never Know', an electro-R&B track (and favourite of many EXO-Ls), featured a sample from 'Deadroses' by US rapper Blackbear, but it soon became apparent that the sample also featured in a song by BTS. Although just an innocent coincidence, this did nothing to help calm the growing rivalry between some EXO-Ls and some BTS fans, known as ARMY.

Ex'Act was received with excitement and delight. The Korean and Chinese versions of the album went straight to number one and number two respectively in South Korea. The pre-orders had almost guaranteed it would be the group's third million-seller, but, within three days of its release, *Ex'Act* became the fastest-selling album in the history of the South Korean album-sales chart (beating 'Sing for You'). And it wasn't just storming up the charts in Korea; the album also went to number one on iTunes in Hong Kong, Indonesia, Malaysia, Singapore, Taiwan, Thailand and Vietnam, and made the top ten in the Philippines, Japan, Russia, Finland, Turkey, Mexico, Denmark, Sweden and Canada. In the US, it reached number fifteen on iTunes, but made number two on the *Billboard* World Albums chart.

> Within three days of its release, *Ex'Act* became the fastest-selling album in the history of the South Korean album-sales chart.

Amazingly, 'Monster' went one better, becoming the group's first number one on the *Billboard* World Digital Song Sales Chart. It also collected nine music-show wins, including triple crowns on *M Countdown* and *Music Bank* (*Show! Music Core* didn't give awards between November 2015 and April 2017). And remember the promise to release a clip of five-year-old Xiumin dancing if 'Monster' won a music show? They were true to their word. On 20 June, Xiumin posted the video on the group's official fan board and EXO-Ls collectively cooed as they watched the chubby-cheeked infant, dressed in a penguin onesie, confidently follow the kindergarten choreography. Clearly, he was born to dance!

Between 22 and 30 June, EXO returned to the stage at the Seoul Olympic Park Gymnastics Arena, one of the largest concert venues in South Korea. They played to a sold-out capacity crowd of 14,000

Comeback stage – 'Monster' on *Show! Music Core*

Talk about a plan coming together. This is how to co-ordinate a comeback stage! They all look fabulous (especially red-headed Chanyeol and blond Kai), the make-up is dramatic and super-effective, Chen and Baekhyun's live vocals are devastating, the choreography is on point (Suho even manages a double dab – it's okay; it was 2016!) and EXO-Ls give a lesson in fan chanting. This is possibly EXO's greatest music-show stage ever.

for six nights – the longest-ever solo-concert run at the stadium. The new concert was called EXO Planet #3 – The EXO'rDIUM. The word 'exordium' means 'a beginning' and, as Suho had explained in the *Ex'Act* showcase, the new album marked a new mature phase for the group.

Those who had seen the EXO'luXion [Epilogue] knew just how much planning SM's performance director Shim Jae-won put into their shows. He was determined that the EXO'rDIUM would be even bigger and better than previous EXO concerts, bringing the performance, the staging and fans even closer. The fans (loyal to a tee) had bought the new Beatlight light sticks; Jae-won had control over the intensity and colours of each one and designed the overall effect using individual seat positions. The stage featured enormous LED screens, pyrotechnics, lasers and strobes, a huge rain curtain and floor screens on the side stages. The set showcased the group's collective and individual skills, and gave them a chance to show their ever-strengthening bond with EXO-Ls.

The EXO'rDIUM set list itself was three-and-a-half hours long, in which time the group performed more than thirty-five songs. It began with a dramatic video updating the story of the superheroes and showing them using their powers on Earth to help humankind, and then the robed members were introduced one by one. As in previous Lost Planet concerts, they next went through a series of song sequences, with short breaks for costume changes during which videos were played.

'Monster' joined the adrenaline rush of the opening section, with Baekhyun's sculpted abs display reliably sending the audiences into a frenzy. The pace then slowed slightly, with 'Artificial Love' immediately establishing itself as a fan favourite as each of the members danced seductively, using a cane as a prop. If the musical structure was beginning to resemble previous concerts, EXO now surprised everyone by taking a seat in a line on stage. Lay and Chanyeol were at either end with acoustic guitars as they performed an acoustic medley, including Lay's 'Monodrama' and an audience-backed version of 'Call Me Baby'.

There was still more to come in this show. Following the success of the festive fun in EXO'luXion, they once again delved into elf mode – this time in pointy shoes, baggy colourful smocks and ridiculous two-foot-high cone hats – for some fun numbers. They played more up-tempo songs, bewitching the crowd in 'Lightsaber' as they danced in total darkness with just the sticks illuminated. Chanyeol, Sehun and Xiumin led the crowd in a chant of the words *gatchi gatchi hae*, 'do it together, together', which segued into 'Full Moon', 'Drop That' and 'Let Out the Beast'. It was a full-on dance party, with Chanyeol reprising his EXO'luXion role on the decks.

Everywhere they took the EXO'rDIUM concert, reviewers noted the effortless way EXO connected with their fans. They could be professional and focused one moment and yet in the next were reaching out and touching hands, pointing at fan banners or just chatting with the audience. On the K-pop website Moonrok, Hannah Waitt wrote, 'EXO has a unique ability to make their performances seem simultaneously spectacular and yet remarkably intimate.'

The only disappointment was another injury to Kai. After two performances, his previous ankle trouble returned and he had to sit out much of the following concert sets. Baekhyun did his best to console him on stage, joking that it was okay because EXO had so many members it was barely noticeable when one was missing!

All in all, things were going pretty well – a number one album, sold-out concerts at a massive venue, music-show trophies – but SM had one more treat in store. On 18 August 2016, they dropped a new single, 'Lotto'. The song, comparing finding your perfect lover to winning the lottery, was another step away from the boyband sound with a hip-hop and trap feel, and a consciously heavy use of auto-tune. And if that didn't grab you, then there was fair chance the chorus would with its infectious sing-along 'La la-la la' and 'Oh oh oh'.

The 'Lotto' video has some of the gloominess of 'Monster', with dim lighting, dark clothes and the traces of cuts and bruises. Centred on the theme of gambling, it also has a seedy decadence: piles of cash are set alight, there's a cock fight, a fast car, a dice table and a girl in peril. EXO play their parts as high-rolling bad boys well, all dressed up in stylish formal shirts and jackets, with the silk shirts worn in the dance sections looking particularly elegant (although Suho's pink hair also catches the eye!). The choreography – in which Sehun's body roll is pretty unforgettable – follows the same theme; and, if the steps are played down, that's more than compensated for by some extravagant hand movements.

After the heights of the recent singles, some found 'Lotto' a little disappointing – but clearly not everyone. It went in at number two in Korea and went one better than 'Monster' on *Billboard*, going straight to the top of the World Digital Song Sales Chart. The promotion wasn't without difficulties, though. Kai was still injured, so they took to the music-show stages without him. And some TV channels wouldn't let them use the word 'Lotto' as it was a brand name in Korea, so for some shows they called the song 'Louder' and altered the lyrics accordingly. But despite these problems, they took their first victory at *M Countdown* and went on to collect seven more.

A repackaged album titled *Lotto*, which included the new single, was released simultaneously. It also featured a remix of 'Monster' and two more excellent tracks. 'Can't Bring Me Down' is a trademark EXO stomp with a dark vibe, superb harmonies and defiant lyrics about the triumph of hope over despair, while the beautifully sung 'She's Dreaming' has not only a luxurious melody, but also words written by Chen – a touching lyric about lovers who can only meet in dreams. Both Korean and Chinese versions, of course, went to the top of the charts and by the end of the month the album and its repackaged version had sold more than a million copies – EXO's third consecutive studio album to achieve that feat.

When EXO took that *M Countdown* victory with 'Lotto' they shared their encore stage with SM rookie group NCT Dream. Next to their *sunbaes*, these teenage debutants looked shy and nervous, which served to emphasize just how far EXO had come. It wasn't long ago that they had come across as just as awkward, but here they were looking relaxed, enjoying the moment, playing along with the audience and having fun together.

This was especially evident in their next escapade, a collaboration with Yoo Jae-suk, host of variety show *Infinite Challenge*. Yoo Jae-suk, now in his forties, had become one of the leading entertainers on Korean TV through popular programmes such as *X-Man* and *Running Man*, and indeed is now often called the 'MC of the Nation'. On 17 September, Jae-suk appeared on the show as part of EXO, singing and dancing to an upbeat, samba-style song called 'Dancing King'. This was released as a single through SM Station along with a video that featured clips of the rehearsals and of Jae-suk joining EXO on stage at the EXO'rDIUM concert as they took the tour to Bangkok.

The song was fun and catchy, and all profits were going to charity – so it was unsurprising that it topped the charts in Korea and China. It also confirmed EXO's status not only as great dancers and singers, but also as bona fide entertainers who had reached out and won the hearts of audiences way beyond the K-pop fandom.

D.O.

FACT FILE

Name: Do Kyung-soo

Stage name: D.O.

Date of birth: 12 January 1993

Birthplace: Goyang, South Korea

Nationality: South Korean

Height: 1.72 metres (5'8")

Position in EXO: vocalist

Sub-unit(s): EXO-K

EXO superpower: strength

EIGHTEEN

D.O.

Korean EXO fans have a special nickname for D.O. – they call him *Almokyung*, a shortened version of the phrase *Alda moleul Kyung-soo*, which loosely translates as 'The more you know Kyung-soo, the less you know him!' He's a man who's full of surprises: a shy performer who suddenly hogs the limelight; a sensible guy who can unexpectedly fool about; a straight-talking interviewee who occasionally reduces everyone to hysterics with one short sentence. That's D.O. in a nutshell: *Almokyung*.

SM Entertainment gave him the name 'D.O.' – a refashioning of his family name Do – and although it's used in official communications, you're much more likely to hear him referred to by his real name, Kyung-soo. In an interview shortly after the EXO debut, he said he was finding it difficult to get used to being called D.O. – in Korean it's harder to say than his real name – and Chanyeol agreed, adding that the others members all called him Kyung-soo.

In 2010 SM Entertainment had asked him to try out after he had taken part in a local singing competition. At his audition he is reported to have sung Na Yoon-kwon's 'Anticipation' and Brown Eyed Soul's 'My Story', and this was enough to secure him a contact as a trainee; but back at his high school in Goyang, one of Seoul's satellite cities, Kyung-soo modestly kept the news of his success a secret.

It was no secret among Kyung-soo's friends that he had a great

It was no secret among Kyung-soo's friends that he had a great singing voice. He sang his way through his school days, making it clear that his ambition was to be a professional singer, and his talent was nurtured by his supportive family.

singing voice, though. He sang his way through his school days, making it clear that his ambition was to be a professional singer, and his talent was nurtured by his supportive family: his artist father, hairdresser mother and brother Do Seung-soo, who is three years older than him.

Even though Kyung-soo was taking the first steps towards realising his ambition, it was no doubt tough for the shy seventeen-year-old at the beginning of his trainee career – and it must have been a comfort to discover that his high-school friend Im Hyun-sik (who debuted with BtoB in March 2012) was starting at SM too. Luhan, who as a Chinese trainee in Seoul probably found the experience even harder, arrived on the same day as Kyung-soo and the pair struck up an immediate friendship; Kyung-soo also met Chanyeol, who travelled home in the same direction, giving them plenty of time to bond.

Some of his other future bandmates, however, did not warm to Kyung-soo so quickly. His eyesight is really poor, but he found contact lenses too uncomfortable and glasses were not an option for a budding idol at that time. This meant that he stared intently at people – a habit that when combined with his quiet persona was mistaken by many as an intimidating glare, leading them to give Kyung-soo a wide berth.

Chanyeol has said that even when they had their debut profile photos taken, Kai shunned Kyung-soo, refusing to eat with his supposedly hostile new bandmate. Kai admitted as much, but added that two days later he began to get close to the boy with the stare. When the group moved into their dorm, Kyung-soo roomed with Kai and the pair have been besties ever since, with enough photographs of their close friendship to fuel a thousand tweets from fans who love to see the pair together.

And it wasn't long before Kyung-soo won over the rest of the group. They say he's much chattier when it's just the members in the room, but there are other good reasons to have him around. Firstly, he is the tidy member: the one who doesn't only keep his own clothes and belongings in immaculate order, but also tidies up after others when the mess becomes too much for him. Secondly, he is an excellent cook. His speciality, spaghetti kimchi, has been praised by many of the members in various interviews, while EXO manager Lee Seung-hwan has called his takoyaki (a Japanese street food consisting of battered octopus pieces) the best he's ever tasted. 'I don't just like cooking, but I like eating as well,' Kyung-soo told *ViVi* magazine. 'I'm good at choosing a nice place to eat. That's why I'm always the [band member] who chooses the restaurant when we eat out.'

> Kyung-soo is the tidy member: the one who doesn't only keep his own clothes and belongings in immaculate order, but also tidies up after others when the mess becomes too much for him.

On 30 January 2012, Kyung-soo was formally introduced as the eighth member from EXO Planet and on the same day he appeared on EXO-K's pre-debut single, 'What is Love'. While his looks didn't create an instant impact like Lay's and Chanyeol's, the voice of the dark-haired singer in the silver jacket certainly drew attention. By time their debut came around, however, many had fallen for the doe-eyed boy and when he nervously made his famous 'superior orchestra' mistake on *Inkigayo* thousands wanted to know more about this handsome man.

Now D.O. has repeatedly said he doesn't like being referred to as cute, so it's just as well that fans call him 'squishy' instead, using it to describe how he employed the common Korean greeting 'Have you eaten?' as a pick-up line on a Japanese TV show; the moment when he had to dance alone to 'Monster' after EXO's second win on *Music Bank*; or when he officially endorsed Baskin-Robbins ice cream with the not exactly unsurprising statement: 'The moment I put it into my mouth it melts!'

There is also the side of D.O. that Exotics once called 'Satansoo' (a term rarely used now as many fans don't approve). This referred to his hilarious, unamused facial expressions and also his ability to be quite savage; to fire off a glance that could kill (often, in fact, due to his astigmatism rather than any actual malice); to react to a joke with a sharp put-down; or simply to deliver a well-aimed blow to keep an over-enthusiastic member quiet.

You can't talk about D.O. without talking about the voice, though. His warm, caramel tones are a favourite aspect of EXO's sound for many fans, and across a range of styles he maintains control and delivers an emotion-packed performance. 'What is Love', 'Miracles in December', 'Open Arms', virtually anything on the *Universe* EP, 'Smile on My Face' and 'Wait' are just some examples of how comfortable he is delivering R&B vocals or ballads.

For a lead vocalist, D.O. has had fewer opportunities than his fellow members to record outside of EXO. This is almost certainly due to his acting commitments, but he has still produced some notable recordings. Chief among them is the 2016 SM Station release 'Tell Me (What is Love)', a track D.O. sang live on the Lost Planet tour but recorded with the writer of the song, SM veteran Yoo Young-jin. A sparse and atmospheric slow jam, the duet brings out the best in D.O.'s voice and the track reached number 12 on Korea's Gaon chart and number two on the *Billboard* World Digital Song Sales Chart. D.O also sang on two successful OSTs: 'Scream' (an OST for his first movie, *Cart*) and 'Don't Worry' (an OST duet for *My Annoying Brother* with his co-star in that movie, Jo Jung-suk). Both were beautifully rendered and very moving numbers.

EXO-Ls have also long recognized that D.O. has a talent for singing in languages other than Korean too. He may not understand what he is singing, but he is a master of pronunciation. His English accent is by far the clearest of all the group members; the accuracy of his Chinese

EXO D.O. ft. Chanyeol – Boyfriend (Live)

The 20,000-plus fans at EXO's Love Concert at the Gocheok Sky Dome in October 2015 were silenced by this awesome 'Chansoo' duet. The beautiful cover of Justin Bieber's hit 'Boyfriend', sung to Chanyeol's acoustic-guitar accompaniment, proved what many EXO-L's already knew: that Kyung-soo could sing English like a native and still bring his own luscious tone to the song. If this gives you a taste for his English covers, you could also seek out the live version of Usher's 'DJ Got Us Falling in Love Again' at the SM Town concert in Jakarta.

and Japanese has also been praised; and his Spanish vocals in 'Sabor a Mi' are impeccable.

Whether it's natural reticence or a 'too cool for school' attitude, Kyung-soo has never been big on fan service. He hates doing *aegyo* (acting cute) and he doesn't have personal Instagram or Twitter accounts. That doesn't stop him being the bias for thousands of EXO-Ls who find him irresistible. His large eyes and his lips, which naturally form a heart shape (even when he isn't smiling), make sure of that.

True to his character, his make-up and hair tend to be understated. He has mainly stuck to black hair, sometimes brown (the lighter 'Call Me Baby' brown is a favourite D.O. look) – although, for a brief time, during the 'Growl' comeback, he sported fiery red locks. Fans would love to see a return to red, but most of all they yearn to see a blond D.O. – there are plenty of photo edits of him with blond hair and most agree it would look fabulous.

D.O.'s hairstyles have definitely been getting shorter, though. In December 2016, he displayed his most minimal cut yet: a lot of forehead and very little fringe, earning him the nickname 'Chestnut'. A year later he went a step further and had an all-over close crop. Some fans took

When D.O.'s photocard for EXO's 2017 winter-special album *Universe* showed just his shaved head, his forehead and his eyes, EXO-Ls had some fun with their #KyungsooPcChallenge, posting selfies of themselves with D.O.'s forehead and eyes over their own.

time to come round to it, but others loved it immediately. When his photocard for EXO's 2017 winter-special album *Universe* showed just his shaved head, his forehead and his eyes, EXO-Ls had some fun with their #KyungsooPcChallenge, posting selfies of themselves with D.O.'s forehead and eyes over their own.

By this point it was apparent that it wasn't stylists who were influencing D.O.'s hair choices, but rather his acting roles. Ironically, for a boy who only ever wanted to be a singer, he is the most successful actor of all the EXO members. Some who stan Kyung-soo originally came across him not through EXO but on the big screen; while at the same time EXO-Ls, knowing how self-contained their D.O. is, have been astonished to see the emotions he displays as an actor.

In 2014 Kyung-soo made his acting debut in the movie *Cart*, for which he was nominated for the Best Supporting Actor award at the 52nd Grand Bell Awards (the Korean equivalent of Academy Awards). In the same year he starred in the TV drama series *It's Okay, That's Love*, for which he won Best New Actor at the APAN Star Awards. Many idol stars are given acting opportunities and open themselves up to mockery from critics. However, it was clear from the start that Kyung-soo had talent. A poll by TV show *Entertainment Weekly* revealed that experts ranked him as the best of over forty idol actors who had appeared in dramas in 2014.

It takes a lot of dedication to combine an acting career with a role in a group as massive as EXO, but D.O. has been prepared to put the work in on both, sometimes flying straight from filming to join up with EXO for a concert. Having shown his potential in 2014, the next few years saw him establish his reputation as a serious actor. He won the Most Popular Actor Award at the Baeksang Arts Awards (often described as the 'Golden Globes of Korea') in 2016 and 2017 for his roles in *Pure Love* and *My Annoying Brother* respectively. The latter, in which Kyung-soo plays a young judo athlete who loses his sight and is then reunited with his estranged brother, was a box-office triumph and earned him many plaudits, with the *Los Angeles Times* commenting that he and co-star Cho Jung-seok exhibited 'a remarkably genuine fraternal chemistry'.

He followed these up with more movies: *Room No.7*, a comedy thriller in which he plays a part-time worker in a DVD store (and has a neck tattoo saying, in Latin, 'He labours in vain who tries to please everybody'!), and *Along with the Gods: The Two Worlds*, part of a fantasy series based on a popular web comic, in which he has a supporting role as a depressed soldier. The second in this series, *Along with the Gods: The Last 49 Days*, became the highest-grossing film in South Korea in 2018 and Kyung-soo has been promised a major role in future sequels.

He was back as a soldier (hence the close-cropped hair) on the big screen in 2018 with *Swing Kids*, a musical set in a prisoner-of-war camp during the Korean War. The role required Kyung-soo to tap dance; it was reported that he trained for five months and wore his tap dance shoes even when he wasn't practising. Meanwhile, on TV, fans raved about his portrayal of a royal in the historical drama series *100 Days My Prince*. Broadcast at the end of 2018, it was a smash hit, becoming the fourth-highest-rated Korean drama in cable-television history.

Kyung-soo had now progressed to getting lead roles on major TV series and increasingly bigger roles in movie productions. It may be generally agreed that he is the best actor of all the members but he is still, first and foremost, part of EXO. He has often stated his commitment to the group and, as demonstrated in his voice, dancing and visuals on 'Tempo' and 'Love Shot', his contribution is immense.

NINETEEN

RESERVOIR IDOLS

The sub-unit is an established concept in K-pop. Multi-member groups, whose schedules are strictly controlled by their companies, can stifle the ambitions of individuals, and the need to share lines among members can also limit the contribution each person is able to make to a song. The beauty of a sub-unit, which might appear for a single track or continue to exist in tandem with the main band, is that it allows smaller groupings of members to explore a different musical direction, without leaving the group or provoking conflict with the company.

Once EXO-K and EXO-M came together, the group had so many members that a new sub-unit was expected sooner or later. 'Miracle in December' had featured D.O., Baekhyun and Chen (they were collectively known as the Gyeonggi-do line as they all hailed from the province surrounding Seoul) and many thought that they would form an independent group. If fans had a choice of sub-unit they might well have picked what they affectionately call the beagle line. K-pop fans love 'beagle' performers who, like their namesake dogs, are energetic, mischievous, noisy and adorable. Most groups have a beagle, but EXO were blessed with three in Chanyeol, Chen and Baekhyun – all 92-liners who can often be spotted messing around.

Another possible trio emerged during the EXO'rDIUM concerts in Seoul. One of the short films shown during the show was called

'Reservoir Idols' (a nod to the Quentin Tarantino film *Reservoir Dogs*) and, according to the opening titles, starred 'Chen, Baek and Xi'. The humorous video cast the three as raucous youths pursued by Suho, who appears as a flyer distributor, a street cleaner, security guard and a yogurt seller. It's a silly and very funny couple of minutes that's capped by (spoiler alert) the revelation that the girl receiving the guys' attention turns out to be Baekhyun in drag, causing many to remark on what a pretty young girl he made!

'Reservoir Idols', despite being a short concert intermission film, is essentially a music video for a fun, auto-tune-heavy, funky rap track called 'The One', sung by Chen, Baekhyun and Xiumin. The same trio appeared again in October 2016 on 'For You', an OST (original soundtrack) for the Korean TV drama *Moon Lovers: Scarlet Heart Ryeo*. It reached number five in the Korean charts and rumours of a sub-unit forming within EXO were rife, but fortunately EXO-Ls didn't have to wait long for the big reveal.

On 21 October, SM released a teaser in which Chen, Baekhyun and Xiumin, dressed as nerdy (and for some reason paint-splattered) newsreaders, announced the sub-unit's name and their first release – except that Xiumin stopped them from actually doing any of those things and we didn't learn much at all, apart from the fact that *something* was happening!

Two days later EXO-CBX, as they were to be called (an acronym for 'Chen, Baek and Xi', if you hadn't guessed), announced themselves at the Busan One Asia Festival. In matching pink shirts and three-piece grey suits, they sang 'For You', to the great excitement of watching EXO-Ls. A week later, on 31 October, they held what they called their 'hot debut stage' and launched their single 'Hey Mama!'.

> On 21 October, SM released a teaser in which Chen, Baekhyun and Xiumin, dressed as nerdy newsreaders, announced the sub-unit's name, EXO-CBX, and their first release.

Those expecting a ballad from the three songbirds might have been surprised to hear a disco track not unlike 'Lucky One'. Over choppy guitar chords and a sparkling beat propelled by hand claps and whoops, the trio spun playful vocals with Xiumin even taking on – and smashing – a light-hearted rap. The video, with its 1970s atmosphere highlighted by bright pastel colours, takes up the 'break out of the routine' theme of the song as the boys lead a fun 'pink' revolution (hence the paint-splattered newsreaders!). The styling works perfectly and the boys, with Xiumin's hair green and Baekhyun's red, look great, whether in pinstripe suits, army fatigues or designer party gear.

Hey Mama! was released as an EP with four other upbeat tracks which had a distinctly 1990s feel, full of clipped beats, heavy bass lines and soulful melodies. Alongside the single were 'The One', the funky track that had backed the 'Reservoir Idols' video; a dreamy EDM track, 'Rhythm After Summer'; the more chilled 'Juliet' with its lush orchestral sound; and 'Cherish', a simple but fun retro pop song. The EP, of course, went to number one in Korea, but also in the *Billboard* World Albums Chart and made the top twenty in Japan and China. That's what you call a successful debut – and EXO-Ls were eager to hear more from the thrilling threesome.

They weren't the only ones making headlines away from the group, though. For Lay's birthday on 7 October, his Chinese fan base took out eleven huge LED billboards in Times Square, New York, to congratulate him and wish him good luck for his forthcoming solo album. However, they were just as surprised when Lay gave them a gift too – an advance release of 'What U Need?', the title track for the album, along with the video.

And it wasn't as if the boys weren't still working their day jobs. Indeed, in November, Lay fainted at the airport due to what seemed like pure exhaustion as OT9 prepared to fly out to Japan for the next leg of the EXO'rDIUM tour. (He followed on after resting and insisted on performing with the group just days later.) Since Seoul, with Kai's injured foot now healed, fans had been treated to the full OT9 experience across South East Asia. The group had already played seven days in Japan, but were heading out again for three nights in Nagoya and two each in the massive domes of Tokyo and Osaka.

When they reached Tokyo at the end of November, a new song had entered the set list in the middle of the boisterous club sequence. The song 'Coming Over' was their first original Japanese number (although there is almost as much English sung as there is Japanese), and its strong disco vibe, provided by a guitar riff, a driving hi-energy beat and swirling brass, made it an instant crowd favourite.

The track was released in early December as the lead track on an EP with two other Japanese songs. These were no throwaway fillers, as both 'Taktix', with its 'Tika-tika-tika' earworm and 'Rata-ta-ta' chorus, and another fabulous dance track, 'Run This', were both gems. The EP reached number two on the Japanese Oricon Chart and followed in the footsteps of 'Love Me Right' by selling over 100,000 copies in the first week.

EXO were now firmly established as the most popular K-pop act in Japan. They became the first Korean artists to feature in the top Japanese fashion magazine *ViVi*, with a different member photographed and interviewed each month from May 2016. And, as if further proof was needed, when Japanese fansite EXOJapan ran a member-popularity poll, it received nearly 12,000 votes (Chanyeol, followed by Baekhyun, were revealed as the favourites).

> EXO were now firmly established as the most popular K-pop act in Japan. They became the first Korean artists to feature in the top Japanese fashion magazine *ViVi*, with a different member photographed and interviewed each month from May 2016.

As the MMAs and MAMAs approached, fans wondered if four *daesangs* in successive years at both ceremonies was possible – but of course it was! The group picked up five awards at Melon, including the Best Artist *daesang*, and at MAMA they took home three, winning the Album of the Year *daesang* for the fourth time running. This was an incredible feat considering that younger groups such as BTS, Twice and Seventeen had all also been nominated. Lay made reference to this in his acceptance speech when he said, 'In China there's a saying that the Yangtze River's back waves will push off the waves in front. I hope EXO will prove this saying to be false and forever stand at the top of the highest mountain.'

'Transformer' and 'Monster' at MAMA 2016

So often EXO seem to save their greatest performances for MAMA, and 2016 was no exception. In two tracks, separated by a potent dance break, they showed everyone watching why they were rated as one of the best live acts in the world. The choreography is breathtaking, carrying such drama and tension, and the vocals still resonate despite all the exertion. Even the moment when Chen has to tie his jacket around his waist to hide his ripped trousers (what a pro!) doesn't take the gloss off this.

Along with snow, twinkling lights and gifts, every Christmas now came with a festive EXO release. December 2016 brought 'For Life', a ballad that may not be as festive as 'Miracle at Christmas' (except for Lay's mention of a Christmas tree and presents) but is nonetheless powerful and touching. It's a team effort, with just a sparse piano-and-strings accompaniment, and Suho, Chanyeol and Kai establish a warm, cosy vibe, while D.O., Chen and Baekhyun allow the song to take off.

The gorgeously shot and stylish music video that went with it featured Suho, Kai and Chanyeol, who play out a romantic scenario about a bracelet that is passed between each of them and Japanese actress Nanami Sakuraba. Does she represent EXO-Ls and the eternal bond between the group members and their fans? That isn't made clear, but was certainly the message many EXO-Ls chose to take from it.

The track was released on an EP in Korean and Chinese versions with four other songs that shouldn't be overlooked. 'Falling for You' is one. A light, mid-tempo number, it is notable for Chanyeol's magnificent 'Ooh ahh, ooh ah' opening and Sehun's 'Yeah girl come on' rap in English, which is either acutely cringey or intensely cute, largely depending on whether or not you stan the *maknae*. Kai comes into his own on the R&B and hip-hop mix of 'Twenty Four'; the slow dance of 'What I Want for Christmas' is dedicated to EXO-Ls as they and the boys celebrate five Christmases together; and the smooth 'Winter Heat' has a dreamy synthesizer-and-string instrumental with an equal line distribution that makes it many fans' favourite from the EP.

> The gorgeously shot and stylish music video for 'For Life' featured Suho, Kai and Chanyeol, who play out a romantic scenario about a bracelet that is passed between each of them and Japanese actress Nanami Sakuraba.

White Noise' – EXO'rDIUM

If you asked those EXO-Ls who saw the EXO'rDIUM tour which was their favourite song from the set, many would pick 'White Noise'. Indeed, many say that they didn't really love the track until they heard it live. The song opened the slow section and there are several different options for viewing it on YouTube (you might even find one focusing on your bias), and many also feature the subsequent numbers 'Thunder', 'Playboy' and 'Artificial Love', in which the moves just get hotter and hotter.

For fans who were paying attention, there was one more Christmas present – but this one didn't arrive until Christmas Day itself. In November, EXO-CBX had released a cover of 'Crush U', the original theme to the martial-arts video game *Blade & Soul*. This was an EDM track with 'crazy about you' lyrics, but the melody and slightly dark feel of the instrumentals make it much more than a throwaway promotion. The music video, which dropped on 25 December, features the boys looking especially smart in black suits with white piping, their hair centre-parted and in more muted tones (Xiumin a fetching auburn, Baekhyun back to black). It even stars a gorgeous fluffy cat that leads them into a dilapidated church, where they look as innocent as choir boys.

EXO had borne hardships in the past, but 2016 had been an astonishing year. *Ex'Act* had become their third million-selling album and their total album sales in the year exceeded 2 million. They had won five *daesangs* and eighteen music shows, with 'Monster' getting the highest score of the year on *M Countdown*, *Music Bank* and *Inkigayo*. Meanwhile, EXO-CBX were the most popular sub-unit in the country and, among individual achievements, Lay's 'Monodrama' had been number one on the YinYueTai V-Chart (the Chinese equivalent of YouTube) for a record five consecutive weeks; Baekhyun had had a number one hit in Korea with his duet with Suzy; Kai's *Choco Bank* was the most-watched web drama of 2016; and D.O.'s movie *Hyung* was a box-office number one.

> The major award ceremonies in January 2017 confirmed EXO's amazing year and their status as a K-pop act at the top of their game.

The major award ceremonies in January 2017 confirmed EXO's amazing year and their status as a K-pop act at the top of their game. At the Golden Disc Awards they became the first artists to win the *daesang* for Album of the Year for four consecutive years, and days later they repeated the feat at the 26th Seoul Music Awards. At the latter, Baekhyun's acceptance speech summed up exactly where the group stood at that moment as he said, 'We promised we'd make you happy in 2016 and we've done that, right? We're preparing to do our best to make you laugh, cry, be happy and feel proud of EXO in 2017.'

KAI

FACT FILE

Name: Kim Jong-in

Stage name: Kai

Date of birth: 14 January 1994

Birthplace: Suncheon, South Korea

Nationality: South Korean

Height: 1.82 metres (6'0")

Position in EXO: dancer, rapper, vocalist

Sub-unit(s): EXO-K

EXO superpower: teleportation

TWENTY

KAI

t is one of the great mysteries of EXO: how can one man be so serious and introverted yet become incredibly sexy and charismatic the moment he steps out on stage? That's Kai – EXO's Mr Duality. Fans even use his stage and his real names to distinguish between the body-rolling, sensual Kai and the thoughtful, quiet Jong-in, with some introducing a third 'character' they call 'Nini' (shortened from 'Jongininie'), the cute and adorable Kai who occasionally surfaces in off-stage moments.

Kai is EXO's dance machine, capable of dominating the stage with immense grace and power. He is certainly among the top five dancers in K-pop and often tops fan polls. He performed in front of a global audience at the 2018 Winter Olympics and has mesmerized audiences with some amazing solo dances in EXO shows. He continues to amaze and in September 2018 posted some astonishing moves to 'Roll in Peace' on Instagram, while in the EXO reality show, *Travel the World on EXO's Ladder*, in January 2019 he learned the complex choreography to Red Velvet's 'Bad Boy' in just five minutes.

> Kai is EXO's dance machine, capable of dominating the stage with immense grace and power. He is certainly among the top five dancers in K-pop and often tops fan polls.

Kim Jong-in was born to dance. He and his two older sisters grew up in Suncheon in Jeolla Province on the south coast of South Korea. When he was young, his parents were keen for Jong-in to take up taekwondo and piano, but the little lad had other ideas. He wanted to dance. By around the age of nine he was attending jazz dance lessons, but then, after being taken to see the famous ballet *The Nutcracker*, he decided he wanted to be a ballet dancer.

Kai's father was incredibly supportive of his son's ambitions, sending videos of the youngster dancing to entertainment companies, and on the final day of the ElyXiOn [dot] concerts in Seoul, shortly after his father's death, Kai paid tribute to his parents' role in encouraging his interest in dance. 'It was thanks to my parents that I was able to learn the joy of dancing, able to learn the meaning of happiness, and able to sing and dance here in front of all of you. It's all thanks to my parents,' he said, before looking skyward and declaring, 'Dad, I love you.'

Jong-in's family moved to Seoul in time for him to attend a performance-orientated middle school and by this time the idol-in-waiting had discovered pop music. He loved the idol group Shinhwa and decided to be a singer. When his father convinced his shy son to attend the 2007 SM Youth Best Contest by promising to buy him a Nintendo console, Jong-in won the Popularity Award and was signed as an SM trainee. He was just thirteen years old.

Jong-in's best friend at the company was another thirteen-year-old (although an 'important' six months older than him) by the name of Tae-min. The two teenagers would practise together, both eager not to be outdone, although Kai has admitted that when he first started at SM he was so impressed by Tae-min's dancing he was more concerned with simply learning from his friend. Within a year Taemin, now fourteen, was making his debut as SHINee's *maknae*, but Jong-in had a much longer wait in store.

You can see what he looked like back then in his brief – but cute – appearance in the video for TVXQ's 'Ha Ha Song', which was recorded in 2008. It was around this time that he was introduced to hip-hop and began to learn street dance and contemporary dance, as well as rapping.

Kai would earn a reputation for being the group's hardest worker, spending hours every day in practice, even taking to the company rooftop to dance in the open air.

When EXO came together in 2011, Jong-in had known many of the other members for two or three years. He had built a good friendship with Lay, as the two often practised dancing together, and had known Suho since he started. He also got on well with Sehun, the only member younger than him in what was to be EXO's *maknae* line, and of course he would build a special relationship with D.O., his one-time roommate and best friend in the band. Jong-in's new name, Kai, means 'open' in Mandarin (perhaps he was originally earmarked for EXO-M), but it did take him some time to take to the name, often accidently ignoring those who addressed him as 'Kai'!

On 23 December 2011, Kai became the first EXO member to be introduced to the public. His profile shots were released and teaser number one was dropped. It showed Kai dancing gracefully while ankle-deep in water and on a night-time exterior set dancing under a spotlight. This bronze-skinned seventeen-year-old, with a mop of silky black hair and poetry in his body, certainly made an impression – fans could almost believe he really did have the power of teleportation that SM had assigned to him. By the end of the year Kai had appeared in three of the four teasers and it was clear he was the 'face' of EXO – for now, at least.

> On 23 December 2011, Kai became the first EXO member to be introduced to the public.

He made his first televized performance dancing as an equal with the now experienced SM artists Eunhyuk and Taemin on the end-of-year TV special *Gayo Daejeon* on 29 December 2011, and went on to feature in almost half of EXO's twenty-three debut teasers. His looks and dancing ability won him plenty of fans, but his perceived position as SM's golden boy also led to some resentment from those keen to see more of their own biases.

Though not a live-wire in early interviews, Kai did win over many of the anti-fans. The other members revealed how hard he worked on his own dances, as well as painstakingly going through their choreographies with them. He was clearly a gifted dancer, deemed good enough to join SM's dancing supergroup Younique Unit, who released a single called 'Maxstep' in October 2012, and dance with SM's elite in SM The Performance collective at the 2012 *Gayo Daejeon*.

When EXO began performing at live concerts or at awards shows, Kai's solo dances became a much-anticipated highlight. From the 'man possessed' choreography (which he helped devise) of 'Deep Breath' at the MAMA show in 2014 to his fabulously expressive solo on 'Monster' and the deeply passionate 'Baby Don't Cry' performance in the water pool for EXO'luXion, he showed poise, power and complete confidence across a number of dance disciplines. Fans had moved on from 'Dancing King'; they were now calling him 'Dance God'.

It was a status that was confirmed when he performed a solo dance at the 2018 Pyeongchang Winter Olympics closing ceremony. Dressed in *hanbok* (traditional Korean clothing), he combined modern moves with Korean folk dance in a precise, electrifying performance that thrilled thousands around the world. And just how conscientious is Kai? Shortly after the event, the dance's choreographer, Shim Jae-won, posted a video on Instagram showing Kai standing on stage two weeks earlier at an EXO concert in Taipei, running through his Olympic dance moves.

The pressure put on the body by such a dedication to dance does take its toll. Kai has endured multiple injuries, most notably having to have surgery on his waist in 2015 (only revealed by Lay in a 2018 interview) and damage to an ankle ligament that led to him appearing on crutches and in a wheelchair on some dates of the EXO'rDIUM tour. His determination to be part of the team despite his discomfort showed his commitment to EXO and the fans.

Kai was originally named as one of EXO's rap line, but even his

I See You – Kai (solo) – 2017 MAMA in Hong Kong

Kai's tour-de-force solo at the Mnet Asian Music Awards ceremony in December 2017 was slightly overshadowed by the controversy over awards and the alleged unfair treatment of attending EXO-Ls. However, taking to the stage in a suit with just a silver chain against his bare chest, Kai seamlessly moved from contemporary dance to hip-hop and ballet moves in a masterful performance full of intensity, emotion and elegance.

greatest fans would admit that he isn't even the second-best rapper in the group. His singing, however, has improved beyond measure and, although he lacks the technique of some of his fellow members, his distinctive, soft, sometimes even husky, voice is loved by many fans. His solo vocal performances have been limited to 'Beautiful Touch' at the Love concert in 2015 and 'I See You' at ElyXiOn [dot] in 2017, but his impressive parts in 'Tempo' and 'Love Shot' bode well for more prominence in the future.

Not that he isn't busy. With looks like Kai's he was always going to be in demand for modelling assignments (on his birthday in 2017, Kai posted the cutest photo of him striking a model pose as a toddler!). In a 2018 poll run on the Korean app Idol Champ, Kai easily ranked as the best photoshoot legend among idols and his beautiful features have graced many magazine covers over the years. Perhaps the most notable was his December 2017 Korean *The Big Issue* front cover, which Kai didn't take a fee for. *The Big Issue* is a magazine sold by homeless people, and people at risk of homelessness, which enables them to earn a small income, and hopefully find housing

With looks like Kai's he was always going to be in demand for modelling assignments.

and employment. Kai's *Big Issue* sold out in two days, and was the highest-selling edition ever.

Kai's elegance and ease, along with his own style of casual but classy streetwear, has made him a natural choice as a model for fashion companies. Calvin Klein, Levi Strauss and Balmain are among the brands whose catwalks he has graced, and in May 2018 he attended the Gucci fashion event in Arles, France, with many newspapers reporting that he stole the show when he modelled a plaid suit with moccasins and crystal headpiece.

Acting has also kept Kai (he uses his stage name as an actor) busy. He made his official acting debut in 2016, giving a fine performance in a successful rom-com web drama entitled *Choco Bank*. In 2017 he took advantage of the opportunity to play the lead in *Andante*, a coming-of-age TV series, and in 2018 he starred as a Korean photographer in the Japanese TV mini-drama *Spring Has Come*. It's rare for J-dramas to cast foreign actors, but Kai received considerable praise for his performance. Many noted how fast his acting skills were improving and this was confirmed by his role as a divine messenger in the Korean TV series *Miracle That We Met*, which earned him a nomination as Best Young Actor at the KBS Drama Awards.

All of the time, of course, he is still Jong-in, whom fans have decided looks like a teddy bear. In the way of such fan crazes it took hold and was even accepted by Jong-in himself. He appeared in a bear costume on the EXO'rDIUM [dot] stage (despite being injured), has a big toy-bear collection, wears clothes with bears on them (fortunately Gucci make them!) and even calls himself a bear. His fans call themselves Erigoms (EXO-Ls are 'Eris' and *gom* is Korean for 'bear') and you can even buy a toy 'Nini-Bear' wearing a Kai T-shirt.

Fans are always hungry for news of Jong-in. On 5 June 2018 he opened an Instagram account and by the end of the day he had gained more than a million followers! Over the years they have discovered that he is a voracious reader; that he has three adorable dogs – Monggu, a

Poodle, and Toy Poodles Jjanggu and Jjangah; and that he is capable of breaking or losing anything. This last point even gave rise to the nickname 'Magic Hands', given to him by Taemin.

Despite their busy schedules, Jong-in's friendship with Taemin has endured. They support each other: Kai rapped on his friend's 2014 single 'Pretty Boy'; Taemin was cheering Kai on at the 2017 MAMA solo dance, and the pair went on *Happy Together* in 2017, the only time Kai has been on a variety show without other EXO members. They also have assembled a tight-knit group of idol friends, including BTS's Jimin, Wanna One's Ha Sung-woon, HOTSHOT's Timoteo and Ravi of VIXX. The idol gang have even come up with a friendship-group logo, which they display on matching parkas.

On 1 April 2016, SM confirmed rumours that Kai was dating f(x)'s Krystal. They were both 94-line SM artists and had been trainees together. Fans of the pair knew they were friends and many had been shipping the couple already, which was perhaps why they were given the fandom's blessing rather than the animosity faced by other idol couples. Critical fans, however, are not the only threat to idol couples. The demanding schedules take their toll on relationships and in May 2017 it was confirmed that Kai and Krystal had decided to part ways.

The Korean news outlet Dispatch celebrates every new year by revealing new celebrity couples. In January 2019 the 'lucky pair' were Kai and Jennie, from the YG Entertainment girl group BLACKPINK. SM confirmed that they 'had become fond of each other' and the internet went crazy. It was big news that artists from two of the most successful K-pop groups in the world were getting together. Fans scoured past social-media posts for clues as to how long they had been dating and realized the biggest hint had eluded everyone. Back in October 2018, both Kai and Jennie been in Paris at the same time; both had posted

> In January 2019 it was confirmed that Kai and Jennie 'had become fond of each other' and the internet went crazy.

Instagram pictures of themselves posing in front of the Eiffel Tower and Jennie had even commented, 'Had the most romantic dinner admiring the Eiffel Tower.' How had everyone missed it?

Kai's fans seemed absolutely delighted with the news, but their joy was short-lived. By the end of January 2019, SM and YG both announced that the couple had split. Of course, rumoured reasons for the break-up were discussed endlessly online, but most accepted that Kai was entitled to a private life. After all, they have come to love both Kai, the super-beautiful idol whose every move is bewitching, and Jong-in, the quiet and sensitive guy who leads a life a long way away from his stage persona.

TWENTY-ONE

IN FULL BLOOM

t was five years since EXO's debut and the significance of the date 8 April 2017 wasn't lost on EXO or EXO-Ls around the world. The group themselves (apart from Lay) were in Macau, preparing for the YinYueTai V-Chart Awards, but as the clock struck midnight they assembled in Chanyeol and Sehun's hotel room to mark the anniversary with a V Live broadcast.

Debut day was greeted by a cheer and a celebratory song and dance, and they soon proceeded to swap memories of getting up far too early on the day, practising singing while running, almost making themselves hoarse and just how nervous they were. What a difference five years makes! They were so easy in each other's company, happy to laugh at themselves, and together they watched the just-released teaser for Baekhyun's SM Station release 'Take

> EXO talked of how they wanted to be together for ten, fifteen, even fifty years and, reading some of the messages they received, thanked EXO-Ls for their love and support.

You Home'. They talked of how they wanted to be together for ten, fifteen, even fifty years and, reading some of the messages they received, thanked EXO-Ls for their love and support.

The messages noted that 'Mama' had re-entered the YouTube Top 100 chart; an organized mass streaming of the debut single was just one of the ways EXO-Ls marked the occasion. Around the world, there was an outpouring of love for the group. Videos and banners decorated streets in New York, Dubai and Seoul; various international fan groups contributed to a professionally made 'Spread Love with EXO' video on Twitter; Armenian EXO-Ls arranged a flash-mob dance; and Chinese fans decorated public buses with cartoons of elfish EXO and animal-onesie EXO.

EXO fan groups regularly organize charity acts to mark members' birthdays, but so many of them used this opportunity to help others in the name of EXO too. These included Moroccan fans arranging a mass blood donation; EXO-Ls in UAE creating a water-well charity project called 'For Life'; and Indian EXO-Ls donating 58,000 rupees to an education charity. These, of course, were just a few of the efforts that took place all around the globe, from China to Canada.

In February, EXO, without the otherwise busy Lay, had taken the EXO'rDIUM tour on the road again. They returned for two nights in the Philippines, one of their favourite places (especially for Chanyeol, who had studied English there in middle school). In their two nights at Smart Araneta Coliseum in Quezon City, the local EXO-Ls were left in no doubt as to the group's love for the country. The boys even remembered the Filipino song 'Hawak Kamay', which they had learned on their first

Drop That + Keep On Dancing + Lucky + Run – EXO'rDIUM in Tokyo

As the EXO'rDIUM concert in Tokyo reached its climax, the boys somehow found the energy for a hi-octane medley of foot-stomping dance numbers, but this wasn't a tightly choreographed section of the set – it was a chance for the group to let loose and party. Shot in high definition and full of close-ups of the members, this video successfully communicates the adrenaline-driven atmosphere and excitement of the live show.

trip there five years earlier. In return, the fans made an incredible noise by stamping on the wooden boards and singing along so well that Suho asked if there was a K-pop academy in Manila!

The tour called in at Hong Kong and Singapore before heading for the final leg – another trip to the Americas. Just over a year before, they could walk the streets of US cities unrecognized, but just how far their popularity had grown was evident in the photos posted of them enjoying time off in New York. Fan shots appeared of members in Times Square, at an art gallery and on a trip to see the stage musical *Chicago*.

EXO'rDIUM drew 6,000 fans to the K-pop-friendly Prudential Center in Newark, before the group headed south for their first-ever solo concert in Mexico. EXO-K had played with other K-pop groups at the Mexico City Arena back in 2014 in a *Music Bank in Mexico* TV special. That performance was temporarily halted when fans threw underwear at the group, so they knew the passion of Mexican EXO-Ls. Having sold out the 12,000-capacity venue, it was now the group's turn to give something back, by adding 'Sabor a Mi' to their acoustic set. The YouTube clip of EXO-K playing this song on the *Music Bank* special had been amassing views and winning over Spanish-speakers by the thousand and those present were delighted to witness the reprise.

The desire to communicate with their audiences no matter where they are in the world is just one of the factors that make the live EXO experience unforgettable. This certainly held true when the group returned to the US to play their final overseas EXO'rDIUM concert in LA. Here Suho announced that 'LA is my favourite place in the world' and, helped by D.O., he began to sing 'City of Stars', from the hit movie *La La Land*, and to imitate the dance moves of the film's opener, 'Another Day of Sun'.

> The desire to communicate with their audiences no matter where they are in the world is just one of the factors that make the live EXO experience unforgettable.

In August, a new reality series titled *EXO Tourgram* appeared on the V Live site. This documented the group's American tour in twenty-two fifteen-minute episodes as cameras captured the group in rehearsal, performance and having time off. Suho and Sehun featured heavily as they explored New York (with Chen) and drove from LA to Las Vegas in a classic American car. As always, food was a constant source of delight, with the boys receiving a New York-restaurant dressing-room delivery, savouring shrimp on Santa Monica beach in LA, and devouring burritos, tacos and nachos in Mexico City.

Despite the absence of Lay and the injury that deprived some audiences of Kai's solo dances, the general impression was that, somehow, EXO had managed to raise the bar and produce an even better show than EXO'luXion. The acoustic sequence, the water effects (in venues where that was possible) and the dance section were all welcomed – as, of course, were the boys' ever more carefree interactions with the audiences. Once again, they triumphantly brought the show back in late May for two encore performances in Seoul. And they really were conquering heroes. The sell-out concerts took place at the biggest venue in Korea, the 35,000-capacity Olympic Stadium (often called the Jamsil Stadium).

When EXO stepped on to the stage at their EXO'rDIUM encore concerts you could forgive three of them for having an extra spring in their step. Chen, Baekhyun and Xiumin, in their EXO-CBX sub-unit incarnation, had just hit number two in Japan with their Japanese EP titled *Girls*. The lead song, 'Ka-Ching', was an ultra-catchy pop song and it was accompanied by another colourful video (with casino images reminiscent of 'Lotto'), where Xiumin garnered the lion's share of the attention with his purple hair and the sharp body rolls won approval all round.

Girls is an EP that can pass many EXO-Ls by as it's from a sub-unit and was promoted only briefly in Japan, but the tracks match the quality of any of EXO's studio albums. 'Girl Problems' has an urban anthem feel, with wake-up opening chords and a fun vibe, while 'Miss You' is funky. 'Tornado Spiral' has a strong instrumental with a rock feel and some more classy CBX rapping; 'King and Queen' is the most EXO-ish track yet as they pull apart some EDM; and 'Diamond Crystal' is a simple but beautiful emotional ballad.

EXO were now established as a – if not *the* – jewel in SM Entertainment's crown, so when the return of SM Town Live was announced, the boys were one of the key attractions. The tour featured massive concerts in Seoul and Osaka, Japan, with EXO lining up alongside fellow SM acts Super Junior, BoA, Girls' Generation, SHINee, Red Velvet and NCT 127. The whole group, minus China-bound Lay, were reunited for a short set, with EXO-CBX also performing 'Hey Mama!'

Much attention, however, was directed at Sehun, who took to the stage with K-pop diva BoA to perform 'Only One'. The pair had been duetting on the song on various stages for four years, but fans seemed struck by how a confident Sehun had come of age. It was becoming a good summer for the *maknae*, who had also been a star turn (along with Suho) at a Louis Vuitton showcase the previous month.

The SM Town Live Seoul concert on 8 July 2017 coincided with some other momentous events. EXO launched new official Twitter, Instagram and Weibo accounts. In 2016, the group had topped the list of trending artists on Twitter, and they were constantly the subject of millions of tweets from fans worldwide, so it was no surprise that fans welcomed @weareoneEXO to Twitter with 11 million tweets.

EXO's first official tweet gave fans the option to click on a hashtag for an automatic retweet that unlocked a special teaser video. This had a tropical vibe, which certainly got EXO-Ls guessing. Meanwhile, on Instagram, the group shared the three latest versions of their logo, each using plants as the EXO letters. One of them featured the bird-of-paradise plant, a bright tropical flower that only begins to bloom after five years. There was a theme developing here!

> The group were soon trending globally with #EXO, #TheWarEXO and #KoKoBop. The latter two were the title of the new album and the lead track.

The group were soon trending globally with #EXO, #TheWarEXO and #KoKoBop. The latter two were the title of the new album and the lead track. Over the next few days came a series of teasers featuring individual members and the look took EXO-Ls' breath away, with the guys in pastel shades – including their hair. Chanyeol's was light pink, Sehun's tangerine and Chen had gone soft and fair. Hairstyles were radical. Kai had somewhat controversial dreadlocks; Suho, a shaggy fringe; Xiumin had gone for a forehead-revealing parting; while Baekhyun took on a red-and-black mullet – one brave man!

There was one member missing, though. EXO-Ls were disappointed, but not surprised. Back in June, SM had announced that Lay would not appear in the comeback promotions as they conflicted with his schedules in China. Many had hoped to see him appear in the music videos at least. In online discussions, fans began to wonder whether he would ever perform with the group again. After all, political relations between China and South Korea had become particularly tense and Lay had successfully built a career in his homeland. However, SM insisted he was still part of EXO and fans would just have to be patient.

What would make a perfect K-pop summer track? A laid-back vibe, some reggae, a little upbeat EDM, some jaunty rap and a catchy sing-a-long chorus should do the trick. Especially in the hands of SM and EXO. Borrowing a line and a tropical feeling from a long-gone classic, 'Shimmy

Shimmy Ko-Ko-Bop', by 1950s R&B group Little Anthony and the Imperials, and a refrain from the traditional children's clapping game 'Down Down Baby', EXO's single 'Ko Ko Bop' does just that, unexpectedly putting together a smooth and sultry summer jam with classic K-pop elements.

EXO Ko Ko Bop fanmeeting 2 x speed up dance

As much as you loved the laid-back vibe of 'Ko Ko Bop', have you ever wondered what it would sound like as an up-tempo number? Maybe not, but you'll still love watching the boys pulling off the moves in double quick time as a treat for those attending a fan meeting in Seoul in September 2017. Chanyeol said that 'Ko Ko Bop' meant 'fun dancing' and they take that to heart here as they attempt the speeded-up choreography. Of course, they pull it off with aplomb, despite being out of breath and stifling their laughter.

The lyrics come courtesy of Chen, Chanyeol and Baekhyun, who individually worked on the theme of dancing without inhibitions. Chen told *Billboard*, 'We gathered all three of our lyrics for the song and selected which lyrics would suit the song the best… Through the lyrics, I wanted "Ko Ko Bop" to have people shake off all their stress and enjoy themselves, just as who they are.'

The sun-drenched video took the chill factor to the limit. In an exquisite, drowsy hallucinogenic trip cut with some classic group choreography, they work the gazes, languid poses and humour (a miniature Suho in a washing machine – come on!). In a V Live special, *Ko Ko Bop on One Summer Night*, shown on 18 July, the day of release, Baekhyun revealed that the scene where all the members were lying together in

'I wanted "Ko Ko Bop" to have people shake off all their stress and enjoy themselves, just as who they are.'

a field represented the moment when they first arrived on Earth, and the video shows the members becoming humans.

EXO-Ls took the cue to search for further meaning, but essentially the video was all about the style. There's Sehun in a retro Hawaiian Saint Laurent shirt, Chanyeol in a white Céline shirt, and palm-tree All Saints shirts all-round. The look even provoked a *Vogue* article – headlined 'Is EXO the most stylish K-pop band of all time?' – in which it was concluded that the video 'continues EXO's tradition of slowly pushing the boundaries of K-pop men's fashion'.

> The video for 'Ko Ko Bop' was given a 15+ rating and some cheeky EXO-Ls suggested it was probably because of Baekhyun's 'scary' mullet.

It wasn't just the clothes. The hair and make-up fitted the theme to a tee – from the fake tattoos to Baekhyun's red brows and silver pearls, and from D.O.'s fake freckles to Chen's glowing skin and the peach eye-liner look. There was so much to take in once you had recovered from Kai's amazing abs and the touching moment when Xiumin strokes Sehun's face.

The video was given a 15+ rating (in the V Live interview EXO guessed it might be because of the suggestion of hallucinogens, explosions or even the display of Kai's flesh, but some cheeky EXO-Ls suggested it was probably because of Baekhyun's 'scary' mullet or Kai's dreadlocks!), but nevertheless in just twenty-four hours it had accumulated nearly 9 million views. Meanwhile, the single went straight to number one on most of the real-time digital charts and, according to Korean media outlet Xsportsnews, reached 155 iTunes charts in the world (including K-pop charts).

Over in Australia, an eighteen-year-old student, Sheryse Skinner, decided to upload her version of one particular hip-thrusting move from the video (the 'down down baby' part) to her K-pop-dance Instagram account. Her #kokobopchallenge was soon taken up around the world in all kinds of locations – even former Philippines vice president Noli de Castro was filmed trying it. It soon got back to the boys, who were reported to be enjoying watching the trend unfold – such was the power EXO were able to unleash across the globe.

SEHUN

FACT FILE

Name: Oh Se-hun

Stage name: Sehun

Date of birth: 12 April 1994

Birthplace: Seoul, South Korea

Nationality: South Korean

Height: 1.83 metres (6'0")

Position in EXO: dancer, rapper

Sub-unit(s): EXO-K

EXO superpower: wind

TWENTY-TWO

SEHUN

The *maknae* has a very special place in K-pop groups. They are the baby of the family, adorable and playful, and can get away with being mischievous and even childish. Doted on and looked after by their fellow members, they are cherished by fans, who always keep their *maknae* close to their heart.

Sehun is the *maknae* of EXO. He is only a few months younger than Kai, but such differences are important! He is a naturally shy member of the group (yet another!) and for the first few years after debut was happy to take a low profile in terms of singing and dancing, although there was no stopping his contribution to EXO's visual appeal.

Sehun often lives up to the *maknae* image of being cute and sometimes brattish, but he is, and always has been, cool and chic. His features often make him look older than virtually all the other members too, and he doesn't always give them the respect due to elders in Korean culture. For these reasons he has sometimes been branded 'Maknae on Top', a nickname EXO-Ls have given him and which even EXO members seem to enjoy.

> Sehun often lives up to the *maknae* image of being cute and sometimes brattish, but he is, and always has been, cool and chic.

Another Korean word that has attached itself to Sehun is *ulzzang* – a term given to those who gain online popularity for their good looks.

When a collection of photos of a supremely handsome young pre-debut Sehun were posted online, fans dubbed him a 'certified *ulzzang*' and seeing them it seems obvious that the cute youngster would be spotted by an entertainment company – how could they miss him?

Oh Se-hun was born and grew up in Jungnang, a district on the north-east side of Seoul, with his parents and a brother three years his senior. He has said that before joining SM he had no interest in singing or dancing and he very nearly evaded being discovered. On more than one occasion Sehun has told the tale of how, when just twelve years old, he was eating *ddeokbokki* (spicy rice cakes) at a street-food stand when a streetcaster approached him. Remembering his parents' advice about not talking to strangers, the youngster turned on his heels and ran away, but the agent was persistent – Sehun was worth chasing – and, after a thirty-minute pursuit, he managed to catch up with him and gave him his business card.

Over the following two years, Sehun went through four auditions before finally being taken on by SM in 2008. He was only fourteen, but fortunately the young trainee immediately found some guardian angels to look after him at SM. He met Super Junior's Donghae on his first day there and they have been close friends ever since, despite Donghae being six years older. Chanyeol started at SM around the same time and took Sehun under his wing; and Suho, with whom he would room for five years, assumed the role of an elder brother. While still at high school, Sehun settled into trainee life, attending intensive singing, dancing and acting lessons. He would spend the next four years perfecting his skills before debuting.

On 10 January 2012, the seventeen-year-old Sehun became the fifth EXO member to be revealed. He was assigned the superpower of wind and kept his own name as a stage name. SM intended to give him the name Leo, but changed it when they realized it didn't sound good when combined with his surname, Oh. He appeared in four teasers, giving fans notice of his immense visual appeal and some pretty impressive dance skills.

Tao, the *maknae* of EXO-M, naturally gravitated towards Sehun, but it was his friendship with another Chinese member, Luhan, that caught the fans' imagination in the early years of EXO. They loved seeing photos of these 'April twins' (both were born in April and they looked so similar that other SM trainees mistook them for twins!), especially the shots of them together in their mint-green tracksuits at the 2013 *Idol Star Athletics Championships*. When Luhan left, many fans really felt for Sehun as the two were seen as being so close.

The Sehun that we got to know was capable of playing the perfect *maknae*. In interviews he often looked scared and was dutifully protected by Suho. He was pampered by the other members, who would offer to cook for him when he was hungry. And he was the one who was best at *aegyo* – an invaluable ability to be cute on demand. Now and then he would also exercise his *maknae* right to be a spoiled brat, play childish tricks and generally trying to wind the others up. Fans loved the freeze game in 'Peter Pan' on the EXO'luXion tour when, for ten seconds, only Sehun was allowed to move, giving him free reign to create mischief.

Whatever he did, the members were suitably proud of their *maknae*, attending his high-school graduation and cheering to the rafters when he won the Artist of Fan Choice award at the sixth Gaon Chart Music Awards. He also showed amazing love and loyalty for them. He turned up at a promotion for D.O.'s movie *Pure Love* and surprised his friend with flowers; he shocked the EXO-CBXers by attending their fan meeting; he sends messages to Chanyeol when they are apart, saying how much he is missing him; and, perhaps most memorably, he was at the theatre to support his leader when Suho broke down crying on stage just after Jonghyun's death.

He also has celebrity friends away from EXO, including NCT's Johnny, SHINee's Minho, and Seungri, the *maknae* of Big Bang. Sehun and Seungri have been friends for years, beginning around the time when Seungri sang while sitting on Sehun's lap at MAMA in 2015. Three years later, they are still close – in April 2018, Sehun posted a photo on

In April 2018, Sehun posted a photo on Instagram revealing that Seungri sent a food truck to the set of a film he was shooting with a banner saying 'Maknae power'.

Instagram revealing that his friend sent a food truck to the set of a film he was shooting with a banner saying 'Maknae power'.

Sehun was named as EXO-K's second rapper, but initially he had few opportunities in their songs and was often restricted to rapping the group's name. Fans began to savour the lines he was given, though, if only for their cringe-inducing nature. His 'E-X-O' chant in 'Growl' became iconic, as did lines such as 'Never don't mind about a thing' in 'Call Me Baby', 'That's right, my type' from 'Monster' and the legendary 'Shawty imma party till the sun down' in 'Love Me Right'. Along with his 'Ohorat!' (Sehun's take on 'alright!') and the self-congratulatory 'Yehet!', which he came out with in *EXO Showtime*, these lines served only to raise his cuteness levels even higher.

In 2015 Sehun was twenty-one years old, had grown to 1.83 metres and had been at SM for seven years. He had grown up. His 'Beatmaker' and 'It's You' dance solos at live performances had shown a confident, talented dancer who delighted fans with jack-knife moves, hip thrusts, alluring poses and cheeky teasing. A year later, in white shirt and ripped skinny black jeans, he took things to another level, sending them crazy on EXO'luXion dates as he mirrored Kai's passionate 'Baby Don't Cry' in the on-stage pool.

In late 2015 Sehun was given his first proper – albeit brief – singing part too, and surprised fans with his steady, deep tones on 'Sing for You'. In December 2016 he sang 'For Life' on the *Winter* album, but it still took him a while to earn the right to a live solo stage and he had to wait until the 2017 ElyXiOn tour to perform 'A Go' and, at the 2018 encore concerts, 'JMT' (which fittingly means 'very cool'). The latter performances also saw Sehun on stage performing his duet, 'We Young', with Chanyeol. Delivered with energy and humour, the upbeat song became an immediate fan favourite and was released, with a fabulous accompanying video, in September 2018.

Sehun – Go – EXO Planet #4 – ElyXiOn, Seoul

Sehun's solo stage in Seoul left those in the Gocheok Sky Dome and even those watching later on YouTube open-mouthed. He had promised to reveal his abs on the tour and, according to Suho, had quit eating carbs and been working out for months in preparation. On 24 November 2017 he was true to his word, taking off his jacket to reveal his chocolate abs in this sizzling dance. It is worth noting that Sehun had also written the lyrics for the song's chorus, but few were really taking that in at the time!

The *maknae* has won new stans with every comeback. Some were with him from the beginning (although the 'Wolf' rainbow hair tested some) or were soon bowled over by the blond elfin look of 'Growl'. He wrecked many biases with the checked shirts and dark brown hair of 'Lotto' and came back for more with the tangerine dye job on 'Ko Ko Bop' and his red-tinged, just-off-centre parting in 'Tempo'.

It is, however, off-duty Sehun that has catapulted him into fashion-icon status. His interest in clothes has escalated over the years and he has developed an easy style that flatters his tall, lithe physique. In a casual look he can rock luxury-label fitted bomber jackets, tailored trousers and trainers, while he can also look effortlessly chilled and cool in a suit.

There can be little doubt that Sehun would have found success as a model even without his musical and dancing ability. He has featured on the cover of magazines from Korean *Vogue* (only the second male Korean celebrity to do so after G-Dragon) and *Marie Claire* to Canadian periodical *TOM*. At the Louis Vuitton resort 2019 show he was hailed as the 'best-dressed man' for the second consecutive year and trended

There can be little doubt that Sehun would have found success as a model even without his musical and dancing ability; he has featured on the cover of magazines such as Korean *Vogue* and *Marie Claire*.

worldwide as he sat chatting to A-list Hollywood actress Emma Stone. Then, in September 2019, Italian fashion house Ermenegildo Zegna named Sehun as their first global brand ambassador since the 1990s.

With his poise and flair, it was only a matter of time before Sehun was offered an acting role. He had played himself in cameos in TV dramas *To the Beautiful You* and *Royal Villa* and, of course, had plenty of camera time in *EXO Next Door*, but his real debut as an actor came with *I Love Catman* (released in China in 2017 but still awaiting release elsewhere), a romantic fantasy movie in which his character was half-cat, half-human – a role he admitted was challenging for a novice actor.

Now establishing himself as a performer in front of the cameras, he had a lead role – with fighting scenes – in the web series *Dokgo Rewind* in 2018 and starred in the second season of another web drama, *Secret Queen Makers*. Arguably, though, his most popular TV role has been in his first variety series, the Netflix show *Busted*. This stars Sehun as one of a team of celebrity detectives solving a fictional murder mystery. It is a great opportunity to get to know his true character and he comes across really well, both serious and earnest (not to mention competitive) – and many non-EXO fans rated him as their favourite detective.

Fortunately, EXO-Ls can keep up with Sehun easily via his Instagram account, @oohsehun, and his V Live broadcasts. They have observed how fond he is of his sweet little dog, Vivi (a Bichon Frise, who we met as a pup in 2016's *Exomentary),* seen hundreds of his *selcas* (selfies) in which he is ever-stylish, never looking less than a million dollars, and watched him earn the name 'Spoiler King' by posting cryptic photo clues to EXO comebacks. He has always been open to interacting with his fans when the opportunity arises, sometimes responding to individual posts, so it's no wonder he has amassed more than 15 million Instagram followers.

In turn, fans look after their 'Hunnie'. They voted him best K-pop *maknae* in an M-Wave poll in 2018 and have given him so much love over the years. Chinese EXO-Ls especially cherish the youngest member, consistently voting him one of the top K-pop stars in the country (sometimes he even beats Lay!). One fan group call themselves Xunqi (*Xun* from Sehun's Chinese name, Shixun, and *qi* meaning 'knight') and love to spoil him. One of the most incredible gestures came in April 2017, when a Chinese fansite bought him a piece of land in the Highlands of Scotland, which came with an aristocratic title – so he is now officially Lord Sehun!

Chanyeol has often commented that he feels Sehun is growing up too fast. To him and the other members he will always be their precious *maknae*. To the thousands who have followed his transformation from shy teenager to confident performer, however, he has blossomed into a witty, talented and exquisitely handsome young man – who just occasionally reveals he still has a little *maknae* spirit in his heart.

TWENTY-THREE

POWER PLAY

I n the spring of 2017, some EXO-Ls played a guessing game for the name of the new album. Maybe *EXOtica*? *EXOstatic*? Or even *EXOteric*? But EXO have never been predictable. The title *The War* was another break from tradition, another example of how the group could change direction. In the V Live *One Summer Night* special, Suho explained the album represented 'our outlook on the world and our lives as musicians so far.' He would even proclaim that 'in a way we are reborn through this album.'

The War was released digitally on 18 July 2017 with the physical album available a day later in three versions. Despite recent diplomatic issues that had made Korean relations with China difficult, SM still released all three versions in Chinese as well. The album was already a hit before anyone had even heard it, with pre-orders of over 800,000, smashing the record EXO themselves had set with *Ex'Act*.

The War put forward an altogether lighter and sunnier outlook than previous albums with almost every song having an upbeat rhythm and a chilled tone. Although the tracks all fall under the umbrella of electronic pop, EXO incorporated so many styles and instruments that they kept the sounds fresh throughout. It's an album that fans like from start to finish, without a single track that's regularly skipped or forgotten.

Among the favourites are the opening track 'The Eve', with its portentous bass and drum beat over which the vocals (with many fans appreciative of Sehun's lines) cast a net of seduction and delicate tension. 'Diamond', 'Forever' and 'What U Do' mix up the instrumental backing, but use most of the members to create harmonies, choruses and even occasional lines that instantly demand attention. 'Touch It' ups the tempo with some seriously sexy electro-funk, while 'Going Crazy' throws down a challenge to the group to use their voices to triumph over the most bizarre selection of instruments (xylophones, violins, bells…). They rise to that challenge spectacularly.

Although it isn't every EXO-L's favourite album, it's difficult to argue against *The War* being the most consistent EXO album to date. From 'Ko Ko Bop' to 'Walk on Memories', the songs and lyrics, with Chanyeol and Chen both contributing to the writing, are all of such high quality. The line distribution is more even than ever and the songs play to the vocalists' strengths, as well as to the group's strengths as stage artists – they were songwriters now creating music with an eye to performance. 'Diamond' producer Patrick 'j.Que' Smith told *Billboard* how SM took potential contributors to watch a live EXO show. 'Getting to experience all of that was amazing,' he said. 'It kind of changed the perspective of what we were trying to create and how to create it, [we wanted] something that would live in that arena environment.'

In just over three weeks, *The War* sold more than a million copies. It was EXO's fourth album to reach this milestone and so equalled the record of H.O.T., the 1990s idol band. Meanwhile, it had hit number one on iTunes album charts in more than forty countries (the highest number ever for a K-pop artist at the time). It topped the *Billboard* World Albums Chart for two consecutive weeks.

'The Eve' comeback stage, *M Countdown*

EXO's comeback on the Korean music shows naturally featured the lead track 'Ko Ko Bop', but the group also promoted with 'The Eve'. After the colourful and relaxed 'Ko Ko Bop', this took EXO back to black-and-white outfits and knife-sharp choreography. The jet-black-haired Xiumin inspired many BTL comments on YouTube, but this is a performance where they all shine. They would go on to win twelve shows on this comeback, including triple crowns on *M Countdown* and *Show! Music Core*.

Promotions ended on 13 August 2017, but by now EXO-Ls had come to expect some kind of repackage. Just over a week later, SM posted a twenty-second video message from EXO Planet. Over footage of a flaming solar eclipse it read, 'The power of music arises when the eclipse occurs.' Eclipses had played a prominent part in EXO mythology, and on 21 August millions in the US would witness a real solar eclipse. EXO-Ls were still puzzling over that a week later when another short message arrived entitled 'The power of music: parallel universe'. This featured the EXO members hanging out in a retro 1980s-style room – and then suddenly they all stopped and looked at the camera.

Fans flocked online to put forward theories of what this meant for the EXO story. They analysed the posters on the wall, the time on the clock, the comic-strip-styled 'EXO Planet' title with its episode number, '2641', the word 'Power' and the new EXO logo – the hexagon-enclosed letters formed by muscular forearms and clenched fists.

The next day brought a longer, sixty-second teaser: 'Power #RF05'. This took us into a sci-fi comic-book world where – in one reading – Red Force had been fighting our heroes for five years and had succeeded in taking all their power orbs except for Baekhyun's (light). Red Force had also transformed EXO into two-dimensional characters. What the …?

SM had been working overtime on the story – or, as some claim, had it figured out from the word go.

While some fans delved deep into the symbols and potential meaning, others listened to the snippets of music and anticipated the forthcoming new single and repackaged album. At the end of August, the focus shifted to the group's Twitter account, where GIFs appeared of each member in comic-strip form, brandishing cartoon weapons and showcasing their superpowers. The music video teaser that eventually arrived on YouTube had the same theme and presented the boys doing sci-fi battle in a cheesy promo that even included a kitten. The mythology was most definitely back.

On 5 September 2017 the music video for 'Power' finally dropped. It pulled all the teaser images together – the power orbs, the space guns, the humour, even the kitten – as the Red Force took on the last galactic gang in town (and came off second best). It was vibrant, with the cute factor pushed to the max, and you just couldn't miss the eyeliner: Chen's golden yellow, Sehun's asymmetrical wings, Kai's face gems, Xiumin's sparkle; even Suho's glasses couldn't mask the blue glint in his eye.

The song itself is pure pop; a catchy and dynamic EDM track pumped full of dance beats with an anthemic chorus. It fits the video perfectly, sounding something like the theme for a superhero film or a game – with added lyrics. It celebrates the power of music and is full of positive, empowering calls to action.

While EXO took 'Power' to the music shows – they would win five more trophies, including their hundredth success and the highest possible points score on *M Countdown* – the repackaged album went to the top of iTunes charts in over forty countries, from Indonesia to Russia to Mexico. Titled *The War: The Power of Music*, it also included the fun disco-bop 'Boomerang' and an immediate favourite in 'Sweet Lies'. This is a steamy R&B slow jam with high notes that send a shiver down the spine. The ever more impressive Chanyeol provided the lyrics, a compelling confession about telling a lover what she wants to hear rather than the truth, which will hurt.

'Power' comeback stage, *M Countdown*

Kai and Sehun both contributed to the choreography of 'Power', masterminded by Asian-American dance group The Kinjaz, and it is devastating. Full of energy and the usual slick, synchronized moves, it also has expression and character – from the EXO-L sign to the arms of the logo to the random high-fives. But what really sent this video viral on YouTube was Kai's extraordinary ballet cameo and, particularly, that wink.

EXO were now household names in South Korea, fêted by celebrities and politicians alike, and they were increasingly called on to represent their country. A hundred days before the start of the Winter Olympics, which South Korea were hosting, on 1 November 2017, a special concert to celebrate it took place. It featured many of the top names in K-pop, including Twice, BTOB, B.A.P, Day6, NCT 127 and BTS, but it was EXO who were chosen to headline the show. Days later, at the Korean Popular Culture and Arts Awards, the group received a prestigious Prime Minister's Commendation. In his acceptance speech, Suho recognized the status this gave EXO and vowed to popularize not only K-pop, but South Korea itself. He said, 'We will be the group that promote and go beyond the Korean Wave.'

EXO's international popularity was already proving useful. It was revealed that the president of South Korea, Moon Jae-in, had presented a signed EXO album as a gift to the daughter of the President of Indonesia, but, more importantly, EXO-CBX had been invited to accompany him to the opening ceremony of the Korea–China Economic and Trade Partnership event in Beijing in December. After a year of difficult diplomacy, this was a significant meeting and EXO-CBX's popularity in China was a vital part of the president's charm offensive.

By this point, their fourth solo tour had begun. EXO Planet # 4 – The ElyXiOn was launched at the Gocheok Sky Dome, on 24, 25 and 26 November, making EXO the first group to perform at the Dome for three consecutive dates. The 66,000 tickets for the dates sold out in 0.2 seconds, breaking the group's own record from two years earlier. The name 'ElyXiOn' was inspired by the Greek word 'Elysium', which means 'The paradise where only the chosen ones can go', and those lucky enough to get tickets were certainly privileged.

In the pre-show press conference, Suho declared, 'When we go on stage, we feel a combination of burden, responsibility and pride,' signalling that the band understood the importance of the occasion to EXO-Ls who had paid a lot of money and waited in line for hours to see them. That's why watching a stage show is to see EXO at their best. They move through varying styles of music with ease, they make even the most massive stage seem intimate and they build an instant rapport with an audience, which seems to inspire them to ever greater performances.

The ElyXiOn saw the boys running through over thirty songs in a dazzling new staging and set. Lay might still have been missing, but the EXO-Ls in attendance made sure he was remembered through their chants. In front of the silver ocean created by the light sticks that filled the dome, the members took to the stage in elegant, military-style black-and-white jackets with Baekhyun's silver hair and D.O.'s close crop immediately catching the eye. Over the next three hours, costume changes found them in smart suits with classic white shirts and ties, in all-white suits, in black-and-red designer wear and, finally, in casual black zip-up jackets.

There was to be no elfish fun in this show, though, as EXO displayed their more mature side, even using a cocktail bar to give a 'jazz club' feeling to the set. The opening sequence of hits still showed off their synchronicity skills, but individual talents were prominent throughout. Xiumin and Baekhyun faced off in a powerful dance battle; D.O. nearly stole the show as he gave a perfect rendition of 'For Life' in English, accompanied by Chanyeol on the piano; Chen astonished with his high notes in a beautiful remix of 'Heaven'; and you could feel the whole audience gulping as Suho filled his 'Playboy' solo stage with sensational body rolls and thrusts.

Others brought new songs to the show. Kai owned the stage with a beautiful contemporary dance, which he helped choreograph, to 'I See You', and Sehun already had the audience in the palm of his hand as he sang 'Go', but the EXO-Ls just went wild when he shook off his jacket to finish the song bare-chested. Chanyeol also introduced something new – a rap called 'Hand', which he had written and produced. It was a song about how he had felt in the past and how he felt about the future. He said, 'I thought of my members and fans when I was writing the lyrics and when I was singing.' It tells of despair and exhaustion, but how holding the 'eight hands' of his fellow members had helped him get through. It was emotional.

It was another supremely well-thought-out and executed show that featured most of the songs from *The War* and *Power of Music* and included another party session that finished with a full-on club remix of 'Power'. And, of course, there was plenty of fan service, but this K-pop term to describe a group reacting to fans with loving, cute or funny gestures doesn't do justice to the attention EXO always give to their fans throughout any concert.

When EXO attended the MAMAs in December to receive their Album of the Year *daesang*, they made sure EXO-Ls knew that they had made history with – and for – their fans. It was their sixth MAMA *daesang*, breaking their own Guinness World Record for winning the highest number of *daesangs* at the awards. Some EXO-Ls, however, were not happy. They believed the voting results should have led to many more awards at the event and were annoyed that the group did not headline the show, with rookie group Wanna One given that honour instead. Many were so incensed that they signed a petition to the government to shut down the event! However, tragic news was about to emerge that would put such grievances in perspective.

TWENTY-FOUR

THE NATION'S PICK

On 18 December 2017 came the terrible news that Jonghyun, the vocalist of fellow SM band SHINee, had taken his own life. All of EXO – and the former members too – were shocked and deeply saddened by his death. Jonghyun had been a friend, mentor and composer for the group, and was loved by them all.

Suho was hardest hit. He was very close to Jonghyun, had grown up with him as an SM trainee and, although their busy schedules meant they spent less time together, Suho still considered him a best friend. Two days after he heard the news, he broke down in tears towards the end of a performance in the musical *The Last Kiss*, and it must have been so difficult for him to take his place on stage as, days later, EXO took EXO Planet #4 – The ElyXiOn to Japan.

At the show in Fukuoka, as a mark of respect, Suho did not perform his solo stage of 'Playboy', a song composed by Jonghyun. Then, at the end of that concert, he addressed the audience, saying, 'Jonghyun, who was a friend, a brother, a colleague, a senior artist and a composer for EXO, has departed this world. I'm sure those who are here are hurting as much as his fans and EXO are hurting. We hope that Jonghyun, whom we love, will be happy and at peace. In that hope, we will sing "Angel", our last song for today.'

The death of such a dear friend had delayed the release of EXO's fourth winter EP, *Universe*, until the day after Christmas. Although they still missed Lay, who released a solo track entitled 'Goodbye Christmas', 'Universe' is rated by many EXO-Ls as the best of the Christmas singles, at least since 'Miracles in December'. A rock ballad with a muted but strong beat, the group's heartwarming vocal talents are to the fore, including Chanyeol's deep timbres, as they sing of their determination to find a lover across the universe. The video centres around the stylish preparation of coffee (could that be coffee-loving Xiumin's idea?). Nothing much happens – Kai is tied up with thick ropes and eventually breaks free – but it's beautiful.

Only one edition of the EP was released, but it did contain a Chinese version of 'Universe'. There were five other tracks, all with sparse instrumentation, beautifully layered vocals and – a point soon picked up on and applauded by many EXO-Ls – all with gender-neutral lyrics.

EXO showed that even after the heights of *The War* they could maintain that quality in their song choices. 'Been Through', made popular in Europe when H&M stores featured it on its winter playlist, is a delicate, dreamy song that just floats by, while 'Fall' is an exquisite acoustic number and 'Good Night' features particularly sumptuous harmonies. The Chen-written lyrics to the soft ballad 'Lights Out' display the singer's poetic touch and 'Stay' has the EP's only rap section, but even then Chanyeol and Sehun keep it smooth.

While the group picked up four more music-show wins with the 'Universe' single, the EP went to number one in South Korea, number eight in Japan, number two on the *Billboard* World Albums Chart in the US and topped iTunes charts in over twenty-five countries, now including Hungary, Colombia, India and Nigeria. EXO were truly international stars and this was further confirmed when 'Power' was selected for the playlist of the famous Dubai Fountain – the

> EXO were truly international stars and this was further confirmed when 'Power' was selected for the playlist of the famous Dubai Fountain.

world's largest choreographed-fountain system. The fountain delivers a spectacular combination of water, music and light that plays out high above the heads of the onlooking crowds and only around fifty songs have ever been chosen as the musical accompaniment. EXO, the first K-pop act to be honoured in this way, had joined such musical legends as Aretha Franklin, Lionel Richie, Michael Jackson, Édith Piaf and Eida Al Menhali.

The members of EXO (with the exception of D.O. and Lay) flew out to Dubai to witness the song's dancing-fountains debut. It was their first time in the Middle East and they were amazed by the reception they received. #WelcomeToDubaiEXO and #EXOinUAE2018 trended and hundreds of fans flocked to the airport – and the fountain – to meet them.

When EXO Planet #4 – The ElyXiOn visited Saitama and Osaka in Japan towards the end of January, two new songs, 'Electric Kiss' and 'Cosmic Railway', had been added to the set. Days later they appeared as two of four new songs on the track list of a Japanese EXO album, *Countdown*. This had been teased back in November with a series of videos, each under a minute in length, which were futuristic, arty and ever-so-slightly disturbing. Japanese EXO-Ls were still puzzling over them a week later when more straightforward images of the members were released, each of them looking every inch the consummate model as they posed in designer wear.

'Electric Dream', the lead track on *Countdown*, is classic EXO. Driven by a finger-clicking back beat, this cracking song explodes with energy, harmonies and hooks. The music video matched this dynamism with spinning camera work, flashing lights and lightning editing adding to the breakneck choreography as the guys skip their way through a post-apocalyptic scenario.

Other new songs on *Countdown* include 'Love You Mo', a song (used as the OST for Kai's Japanese TV drama *Spring Has Come*) with a great rhythm and insistent flow that really plays to EXO's vocal strengths;

'Into My World', a catchy pop song that includes a lion's roar for those missing EXO's animal sounds; and 'Cosmic Railway', a rich, layered ballad with a soaring melody that brings out the goosebumps. The album went straight in at number one in the Japanese charts, making EXO the first international act to top the charts with both their first single and first full-length album.

'Electric Kiss' dance practice

It's just a dance rehearsal. It's not about the visuals or the vocals. Except that, of course, the boys look great in their black dancewear (Sehun didn't get the memo) and the song is a complete bop. But the real reason this YouTube video, uploaded by SM Town, has been viewed more than 26 million times is that the choreography is so sharp it's a wonder they don't cut themselves. The timing is spot on, the moves are precise, the lines are elegant and they *all* look like lead dancers.

On 5 February, a new hashtag began to trend on Twitter. #NationsPick was the way EXO-Ls celebrated the news that EXO had been chosen to perform at the closing ceremony of the 2018 Winter Olympics in Pyeongchang. The nickname stuck and EXO took it to heart. In an interview, Baekhyun said how grateful the group were for the title and how desperate they were to live up to the expectations that went with it. It was Baekhyun who was then given the task of performing the South Korean national anthem at a meeting of the International Olympic Committee ahead of the

> #NationsPick was the way EXO-Ls celebrated the news that EXO had been chosen to perform at the closing ceremony of the 2018 Winter Olympics in Pyeongchang.

games, in front of the South Korean president Moon Jae-in and a host of international delegates.

South Korea made a great success of hosting the Winter Olympics. The sport was often spectacular, they fared well in the medals table, with the South Korean Garlic Girls becoming Internet sensations when they won an unexpected silver in curling, and it was certainly positive that relations between North and South Korea had thawed to the extent that the two countries' athletes even marched together.

The closing ceremony took place on 25 February, with EXO-Ls doing their best to remind people that the Nation's Pick were performing by tweeting #Olympics_EXO 8 million times in four hours! Around the world more than 4 million people tuned in to watch the ceremony as rapper CL, formerly of girl group 2NE1, got the show going.

However, EXO were the main event. Each member was delivered to the centre of the arena floor in an illuminated buggy and jumped off to assemble in immaculate formation, wearing matching white Gucci suits with navy and red piping (the colours of South Korea). Kai's solo dance and the performances of 'Power' and 'Growl' were flawless and were followed by a massive fireworks display. All over the globe, news stations relayed snippets of the act and glowing reports filled newspapers and websites. EXO had certainly done themselves, K-pop and their country proud.

While fans of other groups disputed the Nation's Pick accolade, the South Korean authorities seemed only too happy to acknowledge EXO's status. In April Suho, Baekhyun and Kai attended an official ceremony at which EXO were presented with commemorative medals in recognition of their contribution to the global spread of Korean culture. They had also been made brand ambassadors for Major League Baseball in Asia, which confirmed their international profile.

Some fans, though, were already becoming impatient for news of the now expected summer comeback, but these guys were super busy. In March, they took the ElyXiOn show to Singapore (where Baekhyun

EXO at the Winter Olympics – full performance – Pyeongchang 2018 closing ceremony

Xiumin later admitted that the EXO members, despite all their big-venue experience, were trembling with nerves before entering the stage area of the stadium, but you wouldn't have guessed it as they ran through a faultless performance of two of their biggest hits. The whole sequence, including the breathtaking solo dance by Kai, wearing a traditional *hanbok* costume, to a piece of Korean folk music, is very much worth watching.

sported flamingo-pink hair and Kai responded to fans' banners by saying, 'We are not Nation's Pick, we are EXO-L's pick'), Thailand and the Philippines. Back in Korea many of the members had stage, movie or TV acting roles or modelling engagements and out in China Lay had become head judge on a boyband talent show.

EXO-CBX had been busy, too. Not only had they opened the SM Town Live show in Dubai, but they had also starred in a TV advert for the Hyundai Kona Electric SUV car. With Chen at the wheel, the trio were seen taking a coastal road trip with the boys looking just as beautiful as the scenery. Hyundai revealed a full-length music video with a backing track featuring the sub-unit's remake of 'Beautiful Country', a 1988 hit by singer Lee Sun-hee. The EXO-CBX effect was staggering: the car manufacturer announced they had had to halt pre-orders for the Kona as the response had been so overwhelming!

Having whet fans' appetites with the Hyundai video, EXO-CBX launched their own comeback. The teasers surprised, with Xiumin revealing neon-blue hair that he had carefully kept secret under a cap (some pictures also showed him with a blond look), Chen rocking a deep auburn mini-mullet and Baekhyun with silver locks that made him look like an angel. They were shot surrounded by flowers, a look that went well with the EP's title, *Blooming Days*. This was released on 10 April 2018 along with a charming music video for the lead track, 'Blooming Day', in which the sub-unit perform some slick, synchronized moves, but look soft and vulnerable as they ask, over and over again, whether they can be your boyfriend. It was truly a gift to fans.

To accompany the launch, every day for a week EXO-CBX broadcast a show on V Live called *Mon Tue Wed Thu Chen Baek Xi*. These half-hour episodes took place in different settings, but all featured the trio playing, talking and answering EXO-Ls' questions. The weekly theme matched the EP's concept, which told the story of a romance and featured seven tracks, one for each day of the week.

The song styles vary from the chill R&B of 'Monday Blues' to the wonderfully relaxed Sunday feeling of 'Lazy'. In between there is the springy optimism of 'Blooming Day' (a play on the Korean word for Tuesday), Wednesday's upbeat 'Sweet Dreams' and the slow, jazzy jam of 'Thursday'. The excitement of Friday night is captured in the funky and catchy 'Vroom Vroom', while 'Playdate' is a cute and carefree romp for Saturday. The tracks work together in a stylish and uncomplicated way with the vocals at the fore and completely on point.

> EXO-CBX were clearly as loved as their mother group. The music video for 'Blooming Day' collected more than 3 million views in under twenty-four hours.

EXO-CBX were clearly as loved as their mother group. The music video for 'Blooming Day' collected more than 3 million views in under twenty-four hours and the album topped iTunes charts across most of Asia, in many European countries, in South and Central America, in the recently visited UAE and throughout the Middle East. As for Japan – Japanese EXO-Ls were in for some special treatment.

On 9 May, just weeks after the release of *Blooming Days*, EXO-CBX dropped an eleven-track Japanese album featuring Japanese versions of a couple of previously recorded tracks, and a host of new songs too. Titled *Magic*, it saw a return to up-tempo songs as typified by the lead track, the dance-fuelled 'Horololo' with its chanted chorus and singsong raps. Highlights of the accompanying video included an office setting that enabled all three to don sharp suits and inserts of an explosive dance routine.

The album contained some real gems, including the opening party anthem 'CBX', another emotional ballad in 'Cry' (an OST for the Japanese drama *Final Life: Even If You Disappear Tomorrow*) and a closing track, 'In This World', which delivers a big sound and is a real finale. There were also solos for all three members: Xiumin's retro-bop 'Shake', Baekhyun's powerful 'Ringa Ringa Ring' and Chen's 'Watch Out', a track that sees him return to howling-wolf mode and really highlights his all-round vocal skills.

EXO-CBX played to nearly a 100,000 people in eight shows across Japan in May and June as the album went to number one on the Japanese Oricon Chart. Meanwhile, back in Korea, the sub-unit appeared in a new reality show called *Travel the World on EXO's Ladder*, in which they explored Japan's coastal region of Tottori, but soon the whole of EXO would be back in Japan as SM Town Live was scheduled to visit Osaka in June.

Meanwhile, over the spring and early summer, arguments had raged online about whether EXO could really call themselves the Nation's Pick, but in June 2018 the Korea Tourism Organisation issued a tweet that said, 'EXO has been selected as the 2018 Korea Tourism public ambassadors… EXO will be promoting Korea all over the world now. Please look forward to it!' That was good news indeed, but what EXO-Ls really appreciated was that the Korea Tourism Organisation's tweet also used the hashtag #NationsPick. It was official and no one could dispute it now.

TWENTY-FIVE

UPPING THE TEMPO

By the summer of 2018, EXO were not just the Nation's Pick but the favourites of millions around the world. This was confirmed when an official poll was run on Twitter to see which song should be played at the FIFA World Cup Final in Moscow in June. EXO's 'Power' stormed to victory, beating BTS's 'Fake Love' (although eventually it was agreed that both songs would be played, as the gap was narrow). The achievement dominated social media as EXO-L's expressed their glee at having put their boys on the world stage.

Further proof of EXO's global status came in the same month when 'Monster' surpassed 200 million views on YouTube. 'Call Me Baby', 'Ko Ko Bop', 'Growl', 'Overdose' and 'Wolf' had all received more than 100 million – and that is not including views of the videos in China, where EXO remained the most popular K-pop act. The YouTube views came from around the globe. Indonesia, Thailand and the US made up the top three, with South Korea coming in fourth. The whole world was represented, with Brazil, Vietnam, Mexico, Japan, Turkey, Russia and the UK all in the top twenty countries watching EXO.

And they definitely liked EXO in the UAE. Back in January, EXO had become the first-ever K-pop band to have a song added to the

> Further proof of EXO's global status came in the same month when 'Monster' surpassed 200 million views on YouTube.

Dubai Fountain's playlist. Now they received an even bigger honour: a three-minute light-and-sound show featuring 'Power' was beamed on to the Burj Khalifa, the tallest building in the world – the kind of display usually reserved for royalty or New Year celebrations.

Suho would soon get a chance, on behalf of the group, to thank EXO-Ls for all their recent achievements as EXO held the traditional encore concerts that round off a world tour. The ElyXiOn [dot] took place over three days in July at the Gocheok Sky Dome in Seoul and two dates in August at Macau's Cotai Arena, and were a real treat for EXO-Ls who attended and those who caught up with the highlights online.

The usual The ElyXiOn set list was adapted to fit in a number of previously unseen songs, including the first live performance of 'Going Crazy' from *The War*. It was, however, the individual performances that really thrilled. Sehun delivered an astonishing solo dance to 'JMT'; Chen brought 'Years' to life just through his own energy and charisma and Xiumin, looking super-cute in Harry Potter glasses (which get disposed of as the action heats up), finally had a solo stage with his cover of 'Beyond' that included a brand-new choreography on a stage full of dancers.

If Baekhyun strode on stage looking like a model in his awesome Dior Homme red-and-black suit, he danced like a demon and sang like an angel on 'Psycho', a song no one had heard before. The clip of the performance went viral as fans begged for the track to be released. Then there was Chanyeol and Suho. Looking chilled and up for fun, they sure put on a show. Their duet 'We Young' was a real crowd pleaser, with singing as well as rap accompanied by the most charming choreography. At least fans would only have a month or so to wait before it received an SM Station and video release.

For their part, EXO-L brought colour to the proceedings by instituting their own dress code for the Seoul shows. Having discussed the matter on Twitter, they decided to dress in colours matching the 2017 releases: red on the first day for *The War*, blue for *The Power of Music* and black and white for *Universe*. The effect certainly took the members by surprise, with Chanyeol dispatched to the edge of the stage to ask fans what was going on.

So much for 2018, though. It was nearly August and there was still no news of an EXO comeback. Suho addressed the issue as the show came to a close. He said that, after the concert, fans will only be able to see the group on social media, and he understood that they would be desperately looking out for clues. Baekhyun (who else would it be?) leaped forward to shout 'Next week!' Suho gave him a look and Baekhyun continued '... is August already!' Was EXO's resident prankster just having fun, or had he let the cat out of the bag?

All summer long, the rumours fizzed around the world. Did their new Twitter emoji – a yellow-and-black version of the group's hexagonal logo – imply that something was happening? Was it significant that SM reactivated the 2015 Pathcode Twitter account on July 27, the same day as the total lunar eclipse (and we know EXO love an eclipse)? Would they showcase new songs at the Japanese A-Nation concert in August? EXO-Ls were beside themselves; but the answer to all the above was no. On 10 September 2018, 348 days had elapsed: the same number as the now-legendary hiatus between their debut and 'Growl'.

EXO-Ls like to refer to EXO as having been 'kept in the SM dungeon' back in 2012–13, but there was no fear of that now. They were out there. Lay was wowing America with 'Sheep'; Suho was on stage in Seoul in the musical *The Man Who Laughs*; 'Summer Vacation with EXO-CBX' saw the sub-unit hold a weekend-long fan meeting with Q&As, performances and plenty of fan service; Chanyeol stole the spotlight at the Tommy Hilfiger fashion show in Shanghai; and Kai debuted his mullet-meets-undercut hairstyle in a front-row appearance at the Gucci Spring 2019 runway show in Paris. No wonder they had no time for a comeback.

On 12 September 2018, SM Entertainment confirmed that EXO were recording a video that very day and that a comeback was imminent. EXO-Ls let out a sigh of relief, then began getting very excited:

#EXOComingSoon became the sixth-highest trending topic on Twitter worldwide. A week later, Baekhyun and Sehun, presenting their gaming show *SM Super Idol League*, with special guest Chen, joked that the comeback was cancelled. EXO-Ls nervously laughed along.

On 12 September 2018, SM Entertainment confirmed that EXO were recording a video that very day and that a comeback was imminent.

The release date for EXO's fifth full album, *Don't Mess Up My Tempo*, was finally confirmed for 4 November, with the EXO logo transformed into a motorbike speedometer. The announcement also contained the news that Lay had participated in recording the Chinese version of the title track from the upcoming album, and would also appear in the music video. It was the first time he had featured on an EXO album since 2016's *For Life*.

The fun started on 21 October when SM dropped a thirty-second teaser featuring the members as a slick motorcycle gang, all – including a blond Lay – looking thoughtful and anxious in their leathers. The backing track was a cry of 'I can't believe' followed by series of dramatic synth chords and finished with a pounding beat. What came next were daily YouTube teasers, each featuring a member in his biker gear, while new version of the Pathcode puzzles called 'Circuit EXO' appeared on the SM website, an interactive game that revealed images of that day's chosen member.

The photos made it worth playing the game – even if they were soon posted on Instagram. These were sumptuous, artful and super-posed. They featured them looking tough in their biker wear, dreamy in their soft sweaters and jackets and classically handsome in black and white. For many EXO-Ls it was perfect: whoever their bias, they could die happy now.

On the eve of the release, with pre-sales of the album already exceeding a million copies (breaking their own record), EXO held a comeback showcase at the plaza of the Paradise City resort in Incheon. There they chatted about the album, the video, their future plans (a travel reality show featuring the whole group) and performed some of the new tracks. As it ended they displayed a heart-warming message: 'Thank you for always being with us dear EXOL! We appreciate every single moment with you. Wherever we go will be heaven if EXO and EXOL are together.' Broadcast live on V Live, it attracted more than 6 million viewers (and nearly 2 billion 'hearts'!) and set a new record for the most watched and liked V Live broadcast ever.

The video for the new single, just called 'Tempo', turned out to have very little to do with motorbikes. It did have just about everything else, though: sparkling choreography, exquisite styling, playful humour and, it being an EXO video, a cryptic storyline. Swept over in red and black, lavish settings and switchback editing presented them in an array of streetwear, casual, military and grungy outfits. Kai's revealing crop top, Chanyeol's blue lenses and Suho's smooth polo neck and chain caught the eye, as did Chen's blond locks, Xiumin's flyaway look – with D.O.'s black, Chanyeol's silver and Sehun's deep-red hair being appreciated by EXO-Ls. They had to watch the Chinese version to see Lay's full cameo, as only a few seconds of Lay made it into the Korean version, but it was worth it. He was indeed back, if all too briefly, but looked perfect with dark hair that fell beguilingly over one eye.

The song itself – about the anxiety that a perfect love could go wrong – was a mish-mash of styles that somehow came together into a triumphant bop. It switched pace, along the way throwing in funky hooks, some of their best rap ever, layered harmonies, autotune distortions and even a sublime a cappella from Suho and Baekhyun. It was a classic EXO song – fresh and bold in its attempt to be different, held together by the supreme talent of the vocalists and having at its heart an ear worm of a chorus.

Once again EXO doubled their previous record for YouTube views of a video in twenty-four hours. After just one day, 'Tempo' had surpassed 17

EXO - 'Tempo' on *Show! Music Core*

Hampered by shows being cancelled because of baseball play-off matches, EXO only promoted 'Tempo' on two shows, *Music Bank* (which they won twice) and *Show! Music Core*. Given the chance, though, they displayed an incredibly dynamic choreography, which was equal parts macho, all punching and clenched fists, and cheesy, with dabs and waves. In an interview on the *Happy Together* talk show, Suho said of all their dances it was the one with the fewest breaks, while Kai admitted to being unable to breathe at the end of the stage.

million views. The album *Don't Mess Up My Tempo* had been released at the same time in three physical versions: *Allegro*, *Moderato* and *Andante* (a limited edition, *Vivace*, which featured Lay in the photobooks and photocard options, was released later). This time, however, there were no Chinese versions of the album.

Don't Mess Up My Tempo features eleven songs, including the Chinese version of 'Tempo', with each of the members' original 'superpowers' represented by a song on the album. It's not possible to generalize the reaction of millions of EXO-Ls all around the world, but the overriding feeling was that EXO had once again raised their game and produced their best album to date.

> The overriding feeling was that EXO had once again raised their game and produced their best album to date.

Among the favourite tracks were 'Sign' (reflecting Chanyeol's power over fire), with its hard beat and cool rap sandwiched between sweet melodies from D.O. and Baekhyun; 'Ooh La La La' (which has hints of teleportation – Kai's superpower), with its chill Latin vibe that inspired a mesmerizing choreography performed in the promotions and for a practice video; and the super-funky 'Gravity', an irresistible dance track with lyrics written by Chanyeol to reflect the theme of strength (D.O.'s power).

Chanyeol also participated in writing the lyrics and music of the fast-paced but gentle R&B track 'With You'. Although the song represents Baekhyun's power of light, the rapper said he was thinking of the fans when he wrote the track. He explained that the lyrics are about how people become more similar to those they love and how he, the other members and the fans have grown closer. EXO-Ls were also the subject of 'Smile on My Face' (Lay's healing song) with its message of not being sad when we part. 'We sang it while thinking of EXO-L', said Suho.

The album presented a high-quality mix of styles, with 'Bad Dream' distinctive with its glorious harmonies; 'Damage' flying the hip-hop flag; '24/7', a classic EXO slow number utilizing every member and featuring incredible falsetto from the vocal line; and 'Oasis', the final song, which is like a cousin of fan favourite 'El Dorado', using a similar hypnotic beat and ethereal lyrics.

It was really no surprise that the album gave them a new title: 'quintuple-million-sellers', a feat *Billboard* called 'astronomical in the era of streaming'. The album also went to number one on the iTunes Worldwide Albums Chart and number twenty-three on the *Billboard* 200, and it debuted at number one on iTunes charts in forty-six different countries. It topped Korea's Melon Chart and China's Xiami Music Chart and placed EXO as the first act to surpass 10 million total album sales in South Korea. I think they could consider it a success!

Of course, EXO hadn't finished yet. On 3 December, they revealed a new logo: the group's insignia in the form of a diamond. The re-package was happening. After a couple of teasers, 'Love Shot' dropped on 13 December. The song, about rediscovering the meaning of love, was co-written by Chanyeol and Chen. With a totally infectious beat, this was EXO's unique trap-style laid-back groove. It pushed all the right buttons, with smooth raps and harmonies, a sing-along 'Na-na-na' chorus and

Baekhyun's siren call of a bridge – as well as some trademark EXO sound effects going on backstage.

The video, shot in a glossy and high-definition movie-style, featured an *Ocean's Eleven*-type heist, enabling the members to sport both casual looks and a chic smart-suited style (with some of them going bare-chested under their suit jackets).

The repackaged album, also titled *Love Shot*, featured the single and a Chinese version (unfortunately recorded without Lay) and two other new tracks. 'Trauma' is a superbly crafted R&B number about overcoming the pain of love (try the 8D version with headphones – the voices run around your head!), while 'Wait' puts solo voices and harmonies against a simple acoustic guitar instrumental in another tender and emotional song. These extra tracks were no fillers, just proof that every track EXO now released was to be savoured.

Within hours, 'Love Shot' was top of the iTunes charts in sixty different regions. As well as the expected South East Asian, Middle Eastern and South American strongholds, EXO had now won a place in the hearts of music lovers in North America, in Africa, from Cameroon to Ethiopia, in Europe, from Belarus to the Netherlands, and across Asia, from India to Mongolia. It was truly astonishing – while other K-pop groups were making noise in the US, EXO were taking over the whole world!

> While other K-pop groups were making noise in the US, EXO were taking over the whole world!

The dawning of a new year, 2019, was bittersweet for EXO-Ls. The previous year had ended sensationally. The comeback and the re-package had been triumphant, Lay had proved he was still committed to the group even as his own career took off outside China, and every member was proving their talents inside and outside of the group. But there was a dark cloud approaching: military service.

In Korea, all men are obliged to enlist in the military by the age of twenty-eight. This law will apply to EXO's Xiumin in 2019 and the others in successive years. EXO-Ls will, of course, keep the faith. They supported the group when they were being criticized after their debut; they stuck with them when Kris, Luhan and then Tao left; and they waited (mostly) patiently for the 2018 comeback. EXO-Ls know that this group of uniquely talented young men can conquer hardship yet again and emerge stronger. And EXO know that their fans will stand by them whatever. After all, as they have said all along, *WE ARE ONE.*

GLOSSARY

K-pop has its own distinct culture and vocabulary, so you might find some of the vocabulary and concepts unfamiliar. The following is a reference to some of the Korean and K-pop-specific words used in the book.

Aegyo: A display of cuteness through facial expressions or body language.

All-Kill: When a song simultaneously goes to number one in a number of charts. Usually immediately after release.

Beagle: A name given to hyper, noisy and mischievous K-pop idols.

Bias: A personal favourite of a group.

Bias wrecker: A group member who does something (good) to question or change your bias.

Big Three: The three biggest, most successful and dominant entertainment companies in K-pop: YG Entertainment, SM Entertainment and JYP Entertainment.

Bonsang: A prize given to up to twelve different acts at an award ceremony (less prestigious than a *daesang*).

Chocolate abs: Defined, abdominal muscles that resemble the subdivided parts of a chocolate bar.

Comeback: When an artist releases a new single, mini-album or album and promotes them on TV.

Daesang: The prestigious 'Grand Prize' at a Music Awards, awarded for artist, song or album of the year.

Debut: An act's first performance (usually on TV). The official launch of an act is a crucial opportunity to make an impression on the watching public.

Fandom: Short for 'fan domain', it includes everything that goes on in the fan community, from fan clubs to online forums.

Hallyu: Refers to the 'Korean Wave'; a growing interest in South Korean culture that has spread worldwide in the twenty-first century.

Hoobae: People with less experience at work, school or as trainees.

Hyung: A Korean mark of respect spoken by a man to an older close male friend or brother.

It can stand alongside or be used in conjunction with the name, such as 'Jun-myeon-Hyung'.

Idol: An artist in mainstream and commercial K-pop.

Ipdeok: To become a fan. *Ipdeok* idols attract people into a fandom.

Line: A word used to link together group members or friends. Often used with a year (e.g. 95-line) to group individuals born in that year or with a group designation such as 'rap line' or 'vocal line'.

Maknae: The youngest member; as such they are allowed to be silly or mischievous and are expected to be cute.

Nugu: Meaning a 'nobody', it is used in K-pop to insult unpopular groups or idols.

Rookie: A group which has debuted but is still in their first – or sometimes, second – year.

Sasaeng: A zealous fan who is considered over-obsessive, often stalking and invading the privacy of their idols.

Selca: A selfie.

Ship: A romantic or platonic relationship.

Shipping: Fans' (usually imaginative) pairing of idols or characters in romantic or platonic relationships.

Solo stage: Part of a concert where a member performs a solo song or dance.

Stan: A passionate fan. Also used as a verb, as in 'You should stan Kai.'

Streetcasting: Entertainment company agents scouting for potential trainees in public areas.

Sub-unit: A small group formed from the members of a larger group. It can be a one-off project or an on-going group such as EXO-CBX.

Sunbae: People with more experience at work, school or as trainees.

Trainee: A young performer signed to an entertainment company in order to train in dance, singing and other performing arts with a view to becoming an idol.

Ulzzang: Meaning 'good looking', it is used to refer to those who gain a reputation for their beauty through photographs uploaded online.

Visual: The group member who is considered the most beautiful or a member who is included in the group because of their looks.

Weibo: A Chinese social media site similar to (but with twice as many users as) Twitter.

ACKNOWLEDGEMENTS

It's been great fun researching and writing the story of such an interesting and talented group as EXO, but I couldn't have done it without the support of many others. My thanks go to Becca Wright for her enthusiasm, editing and help throughout the project, and to Louise Dixon, Monica Hope, Richard Rosenfeld, Mark Bracey, Ana Bjezancevic, Alara Delfosse, Evangeline Sellers and everyone else at Michael O'Mara Books. I would also like to thank Nora Besley for her constant updates on EXO and K-pop in general, Lisa Hughes for her diligent reading of the drafts, and the thousands of EXO-Ls around the world who continue to document and translate every detail of the group's incredible journey.

PICTURE CREDITS

INDEX